500 TIPS FOR STUDENTS

𝔹

To my son, Angus.

*In the hope that he may read
the advice that he won't listen to . . .*

500
TIPS FOR
STUDENTS

Phil Race

BLACKWELL
Oxford UK & Cambridge USA

Copyright © Standing Conference on Educational Development 1992

First published 1992
Reprinted 1993 (twice), 1994, 1996

Blackwell Publishers Ltd
108 Cowley Road
Oxford OX4 1JF
UK

British Library Cataloguing in Publication Data

A CIP catalogue record for this book is available from the British Library.

ISBN 0–631–18851–7

Typeset in 11 on 13 pt Palatino by Hope Services (Abingdon) Ltd.
Printed in Great Britain by T.J. Press (Padstow) Ltd, Padstow, Cornwall.

This book is printed on acid-free paper.

Contents

Acknowledgements

I am grateful to David Baume (Chair of SCED) for suggesting several of the topics covered in this book. I am also grateful to countless students – past and present – upon whose experience this book is based.

Phil Race, July 1991

The cartoons have been drawn by Edwin Rostron, a teenage student who is also a freelance cartoonist and designer based in Newcastle upon Tyne. He can be contacted through SCED.

About this Book

Success in your course depends not so much on how much you know, but on how well you use it. Success is really a measure of how well-developed your study skills are. This collection lists ten tips on fifty-one topics. It has been developed over a number of years with the help of many students and was marketed in pilot form by SCED last year. Now, the final version is being published in association with Blackwell Publishers to make its valuable advice available to students everywhere.

For each topic, I have tried to list the ten most important pieces of advice. Each topic is intended to be complete in itself, though you'll find connections between many of the ideas under the various headings.

You can use this book in several ways, including:

- **consult it selectively for whichever topic is important at a given time**
- **work through the whole book systematically, choosing suggestions which may help you in particular**
- **experiment with ideas you haven't yet used – see if they work for you**
- **look at each topic and decide which *one* idea is the most useful one for you in particular**

- use the book as a means of finding out your strengths and weaknesses
- use the book with fellow students, trying out suggestions then sharing your experiences
- improve on the suggestions (and let me know your improvements)
- apply the approach and work out 'ten tips' for new topics (and let me know if you would like them included in the next edition of this book).

Taking Charge of your Studies

Looking back at early stages in your studies, you probably feel that you were often doing things to other people's specifications, and in ways laid down by other people. In higher education you can take charge of most of this for yourself. Now's your chance to develop yourself as a self-motivating person.

1 **Make your own reasons for studying.** 'Because other people expect things of you' is one reason for studying, but if you really want to take charge of your studies, it's best that you have strong reasons of your own.

2 **Don't let other people take charge.** You'll never get the self-satisfaction which comes with being in charge of your own studies if you're constantly having to meet other people's deadlines. Make your own (earlier) deadlines – and live up to them.

3 **Make your own agendas.** Admittedly, the agenda for your studies is dictated to some extent by other people, for example, through the syllabus you're studying. However, **you** can decide exactly what you're going to tackle, and when, and in what order.

4 **Build in self-assessment.** In due course, other people will assess your work one way or another, but this doesn't prevent you from doing a lot of self-assessment

first. When you've practised self-assessment, other kinds of assessment become a lot less daunting.

5   **Work out the assessment criteria for yourself.** You've got plenty of clues – old exam papers, past assignments, clues from your tutors, syllabus objectives, and your notes and books. If you can formulate a good set of assessment criteria for yourself, you'll have no problems matching up to other people's assessment criteria in due course.

6   **Decide your own targets.** You'll frequently be working with other people's targets – particularly what to learn and when to learn it – but that's no reason for avoiding the business of making your own targets too. Make your own targets a little more rigorous than other people's.

7   **Work out what your resources are.** These include your study materials, your tutors, and your fellow students. If you regard tutors as resources, rather than as a source of pressure on you, you'll make better use of them. If you regard fellow students as resources rather than competitors, you'll derive more benefit from them.

8   **Use all the feedback you can get.** When you get back assessed work, even if there are critical comments or low grades – don't allow yourself to be 'switched-off' by them. Turn critical comment to your advantage – turn it into a positive resource.

9   **Adjust your plans frequently.** Changing your plans in the light of fresh information is a sign of strength, not weakness. At any one time, have a list of things you intend to do in the immediate future, with an order of priority. Review the order of priority as circumstances develop.

10 **Make each study task your own.** For each task, decide not only **what** you intend to do and **when** you

2

intend to complete it, decide also **why** you're doing the task (your own reasons) and **what** you personally intend to get out of doing it.

The Week Before you Start your Course

Just before you start your course can be a time of high emotion – whether it's fear of the unknown or unbridled excitement. There are useful and constructive things you can do in the days leading up to the start of a new course.

1 **Collect together all your information – and read it!** Information such as is contained in the Prospectus, syllabus options, travel information, accommodation information – all needs to be read before you set off. It makes your task a lot more straightforward if you've quietly anticipated the decisions you'll need to make in the early days of your new course.

2 **Analyse your strengths.** Make a list of things you know you're good at. This helps to build your confidence – and helps you anticipate ways you can apply your strengths to new situations ahead.

3 **Analyse your weaknesses too!** Make a list of things you know you're *not yet* good at. Doing this helps you to become more receptive to ways round any weaknesses.

4 **Look at the opportunities ahead.** Work out good answers to the following questions: *'Why am I taking this course?'*, *'What's in it for me?'*, *'How will it improve the rest of my life?'*. This is your chance to prime your

self with some firm reasons for keeping going when the going gets tough.

5 **Anticipate any 'threats'.** Being prepared is more than being halfway towards meeting challenges and difficulties.

6 **Polish up what you already can do.** Admission to your new course will have depended on 'prerequisite' knowledge and skills. Make sure that the more important skills are at your fingertips – not buried in the distant past.

7 **Prepare your own agenda.** Normally, it will be some weeks – even months – before the pace of your new course 'hots up'. If you've got your own agenda of things you intend to do, you can put to good use the relatively easy time at the beginning of the course.

8 **Make a list of things you intend to find out in the first week of the course.** There may be many questions racing around in your mind – once you've crystallized them into a list, you don't have to try keeping them all in your mind.

9 **Think 'positive'.** Regard any difficulty you may encounter as an opportunity to develop new competences.

10 **Expect change and uncertainty.** Coping with change is one of the most useful life-skills. Develop your patience and flexibility, and maintain your determination to learn as much as you can from each situation you encounter in the new course.

Finding out where you're at

'**How am I doing?**' is a question which is on every student's mind. If you address this question consciously throughout your studies, there's far less chance of getting sudden 'shocks' after other people (for example examiners) give you their assessments of how you're doing. The following suggestions show some ways you can find out how you're doing as a day-to-day part of your approach to your studies.

1   **Accept that there's no 'bad news'.** One of the reasons that many students don't try to find out where they're at is that they fear finding out that they're not doing well enough. In fact, finding this out early is 'good news' – there's still plenty of opportunity to do something about it.

2   **Don't wait for other people to tell you.** Sooner or later other people will tell you how you're doing – for example exam results or marked coursework. This can be too late. The more you can find out about how you're doing **before** formal assessments, the better you can fine-tune your studying to overcome any problems or difficulties.

3   **Work out the criteria for yourself.** You can get many 'clues' to the benchmarks you need to live up to.

Constantly ask yourself 'what exactly could I be expected to become able to do with this?' and keep track of the things you **can't yet do** as well as the things you can do.

4 **Compare yourself with others.** There's no better way of finding out how you're doing than to work **with** fellow students rather than compete privately against them. Finding out what other people can do helps you build a valuable frame of reference, so you can put the things you can do (and can't yet do) into a sensible perspective.

5 **Practise the things you can do.** It's one thing knowing how to do something – it's another thing being able to do it at any time when asked. Much depends on **how often** you've tried to do something.

6 **Search for the things you can't yet do.** If you know what you can't yet do – it's far better than finding out too late. Make lists of questions about the things you can't yet do, and gradually find out how to do them. Ask your tutors to explain anything that really puzzles you. Ask fellow students to explain things to you – when people have just learned something, they often explain it more clearly than someone who has known it for a long time.

7 **Search for things you've forgotten.** We all forget most of the things we learn! But re-learning them takes much less time. The more often you've forgotten something, the less likely it becomes that you'll forget it again.

8 **Pay particular attention to feedback comments from tutors.** When you hand in some coursework for marking, the score or grade you receive is often far less important than the comments your tutor may have written on your work. These comments can give you valuable insight into how to try the next piece of work – and how to tackle similar exam questions.

9 **Assess yourself.** Practise having a go at projects or old exam questions, then work out how you would have done if it was being assessed. Look particularly at the things you didn't get right – and the things you missed out.

10 **Get other people to quiz you.** Use short, sharp questions you design yourself. Any longer question can be answered successfully if you know how to handle a range of related short sharp questions. Other people quizzing you gives a useful and accurate answer to the question 'how am I doing?'

Exploring How You Learn

You've been learning all your life – but you may not have had cause to think back and analyse **how** you learn. You probably learn in a number of different ways, depending on what you're learning, and how your learning is to be demonstrated or measured. The following suggestions can help you find out more about how your learning happens – leading to the chance for you to exploit things that work well for you. For the questions below you'll need something to write on (this page will do) and a pen or pencil.

1 Think of something you **know you're good at**. It doesn't matter what. Jot down something now.
2 Next, jot down a few words about **how** you became good at whatever it was. Do this now, before reading '3' below.
3 Compare the way you learned the thing you're good at with the following common answers to the question **'how?'**: *'by practising it'; 'by trial and error'; 'by getting it wrong at first and learning what went wrong and why'*. Not many people report becoming good at something just by listening to other people talking about it – or by reading about it. Most learning happens through **'doing'** of one form or another. Thinking of your present studies, make a list of the

sorts of 'doing' which are most likely to help you con-solidate your learning.

4   Now still thinking of the thing you chose that you're good at, jot down a few words about the **evidence** you can call on that you're good at it. Then look at '5' below and we'll analyse the sort of evidence you may have drawn on.

5   The sort of evidence you're likely to have chosen is probably something you **do** or **have done**. It's not just a matter of knowing a lot, or having a skill – it's to do with ways of **showing** your knowledge or skills. Thinking of the things you need to learn in your stud-ies, work out the sort of **evidence** that in due course you'll be expected to demonstrate. The more you know about such evidence, the more you can prepare to demonstrate it when required.

6   Now think of something about yourself you **feel good about**. Jot it down. It could be a personal quality, or something you're proud of. When you've jotted some-thing down, move to '7' below and we'll look further into it.

7   Thinking of something you feel good about, jot down a few words to explain **how you know** you can feel good about it. What sorts of **evidence** have you to support your feelings?

8   The most common answers to '7' above mention 'other people' – for example 'other people tell me', 'feedback received from other people', and so on. It's important to feel good about the results of your studying – and other people can be the key to developing the confidence and satisfaction which comes with success-ful learning.

9   Thinking ahead to studying ahead of you, make a plan that will help you learn by doing **and** get regular feed-back from other people on your learning. This can help

you learn efficiently **and** help you develop positive feelings about the way your learning is going.

10 Talk through the questions and ideas above with some other people. You could choose fellow students, friends, relatives – almost anyone. See if you can involve some other people in your plans for effective studying – and help them by supporting them in their own plans.

Organizing Your Studies

1   **Decide you're not going to allow yourself to drown!** If you're not well organized, the demands you face can seem like an uncontrolled tide, and you may feel yourself getting submerged. However, once you've made the conscious decision to stay **in charge** of the organization of your studies, you will be in a much stronger position to 'ride the waves'.

2   **Make lists.** Don't just make 'bland lists' containing unhelpful aims such as 'learn all of Ms Jones' notes'. Make long lists – but of short, specific goals. This means that you can achieve a goal or two frequently, and **cross them off your list**. It's very satisfying to delete things from your agenda when you've done them.

3   **Add each task you're given to your list**. Invent a system for prioritizing the items on your list – not in terms of deadlines such as hand-in dates, but in order of **importance**. By all means pay attention to deadlines – but pay even more attention to getting down to studying which you know is important in the longer term.

4   **Review your lists regularly.** (This only takes a few minutes now and then.) When you find that something is becoming more important, upgrade its priority on your list. Set your own target dates for achieving things

Make lists

on your list – choosing dates that are well ahead of any 'external' deadlines such as hand-in dates.

5 **Build variety into your studying.** For example, if you're spending an evening studying, don't just plod on with one single task for the whole time. Spend a little of the time revising something, a little planning a future task, a little pressing on with some tasks already in progress, and a little reading around your subjects. 'A change is as good as a rest' – you'll get more efficiency if your brain has a variety of exercises during an evening rather than a monotonous long plod through one task.

6 **Use 'spare' bits of time.** There are 'odd minutes free' spread through the day of even the busiest of people. Use some of these 'odd minutes' to do small tasks – for example jotting down two important ideas from one of last week's classes. You may be surprised how productive these little bits of time can prove – our

concentration spans are short – and easily maintained in these little 'bursts' of activity.

7   **Have something with you that you can do – everywhere!** There's no point carrying all your books and notes around with you all day – but it's very useful to have something **small** with you (such as a pocket book or card containing some key information you're learning). Also, when planning a major task like an essay, it's useful to carry your essay-plan around with you for a few days, gradually sorting out your ideas and noting key words and phrases on your plan.

8   **Don't just work in your 'favourite place'.** Most people have preferred working places – for example the library or study-bedroom. However, if you **only** work when in your preferred place, it becomes an easy excuse for **not working** everywhere else.

9   **Right from the start – prepare for the way your learning will be assessed.** If your course relies on exams, start practising answering questions as soon as you've covered enough to answer some questions on! You should be able to start answering questions by the end of your first week.

10 **Work with fellow students when you can.** Working on your own, sadly it's possible to sit at your desk for hours without much learning happening. When you're part of a productive 'learning syndicate', your chances of idly daydreaming are dramatically reduced. Every time you explain something to a fellow-student, **you** do some valuable learning yourself.

Where to Study

'Time-management' is a subject mentioned frequently – organizations pay out considerable sums sending staff on time-management courses. Little is ever said about **'place-management'** but it is just as important when it comes to studying. The following questions and suggestions may help you to become better at 'place-management'.

1 Have you an **'ideal'** place to study? Jot down a few features of your personal 'ideal' learning environment before reading on.

2 When asked where the best place to study is, many people say 'the library' or 'at home' or 'in my study-bedroom'. The danger is that having a favourite place to study can become your **excuse** for doing no work at all in any of the remaining places.

3 Strike a balance between **efficiency** and **opportunity**. If (for example) you work best in your study-bedroom, it's probable that your efficiency there will be high. However, you're not always there! It's worth doing some of your studying in other places as well – even if you're not quite so efficient elsewhere.

4 **Match the task to the place.** For some tasks you need plenty of room to spread out. For some tasks you may need specialized equipment – drawing boards,

computers, and so on. Other tasks you can do with a book or notepad perched on your knee.

5 **Use odd places!** Suppose you picked one important page from your notes, and took it outside, under an umbrella, in the rain, at night, with a torch – for five minutes. You'd **remember** the learning you did in that five minutes for a very long time. Your learning would be linked to the (memorable) circumstances surrounding the event.

6 **Have something to learn with you.** By now, you'll be getting the message – the place to learn is where you are – anywhere – everywhere. If you've nothing with you, you've got the perfect excuse to do no learning. Don't give yourself that luxury.

7 **Don't spend time tidying up before starting learning.** Tidy up half-an-hour later. Then, as you rearrange your environment, your brain will be pro-

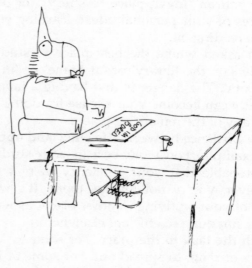

Stare at the ceiling

16

cessing the ideas you've been studying. (If you tidy up first, all you're really thinking about is tidying up – and how long you can put off the dreadful moment of starting to think.)

8 **Don't be too fussy about your environment.** Some people *prefer* to study in absolute silence – others in a din. Some like a comfortable chair – others perch or sprawl. Develop your skills to concentrate **despite** the surroundings – these skills are very valuable throughout life.

9 **Stare at the ceiling** – or out of the window – and so on! Don't regard this sort of 'escape' as a forbidden pleasure – regard it as a necessity. Our brains need time to reflect on ideas we've just come across – but don't reflect for *too* long at a time!

10 Combining all of the above suggestions, adopt the philosophy that the place to study is **where you are**.

Task Management

Although good time-management skills are very valuable, good 'task-management' skills are even more important. 'Task-management' is about the **quality** of the work you do, and about the **contribution** of the learning payoff of the various tasks to your success. The following suggestions should help you to keep a sensible balance between tasks you're given, and tasks you decide to set yourself.

1   Keep an eye on **what each task is worth** in terms of its contribution to your overall course assessment. It's sensible to spend proportionate amounts of your time and energy accordingly. Remember that *most* of the marks may be associated with the quality and quantity of *revision* that you do – make sure that you address revision alongside your day-to-day tasks, rather than leaving it all for 'when you've got time'.

2   Don't be preoccupied with **'urgent'** tasks. If you spend all your time and energy on an urgent task, it will simply get replaced in due course with another 'urgent' one. Try to make an early start on all tasks, so that as few as possible ever become urgent. A useful maxim is *'before doing any urgent task, spend 30 minutes doing something that isn't urgent'*. The urgent task will still get done.

3 Give priority to tasks where there is a **'high learning payoff'**. Don't simply be satisfied with finishing the tasks – try to find ways of bringing together the things you learned while doing them.

4 **Have several tasks 'on the go' at any time.** If you just have a single task, it's all too easy to find reasons (excuses) for not getting down to it. When you have several things in progress, at least you can get down to something else when you feel the need to avoid doing one particular task. **Make lists** of the tasks you're working on – it's highly satisfying to cross things off your list when they're completed!

5 **Use deadlines.** Often, you'll have other people's deadlines to work to – but **set your own personal deadlines** (earlier than other people's deadlines). The increased self-satisfaction which comes with working ahead of schedule will give you confidence – and this increases the quality of the tasks you do.

6 **Choose your own agenda of tasks** alongside the work which is set as part of your course. For example, it is important to spend a fair amount of your time simply consolidating your command of things you've already learned – rather than just pressing ahead doing the work you're given.

7 **Avoid backlogs.** Many students suffer by accumulating a backlog of course work (for example writing up practical work), and end up having to tackle such backlogs at a time when a much more productive task would be structured revision and preparation for exams.

8 **Don't spend too long on any task.** Suppose a particular task is worth 10 marks: if you spend a *reasonable* time on it you may score 7 or 8 of the marks; if you spend a great deal of time on it you're unlikely to score more than 9 marks. It's just not worth the extra time.

The extra time would be far better used for sponta-neous consolidation of things you've already learned.

9 **Don't be a perfectionist.** You've got the rest of your life to be a perfectionist if you're inclined that way. Meanwhile, good task management is about doing a *reasonable* amount of work on each task, and making sure that you address *all* the tasks you need to do. Perfectionists often end up with backlogs of impor-tant tasks – due to doing a small number of tasks very well indeed.

10 **Don't struggle for too long – do something else meanwhile.** A task which seems impossible today may seem simple in a month's time, when you've gathered the necessary information and experience upon which to structure your approach to the task. The real danger with getting 'stuck' on a task is the queue of other tasks which may accumulate as you struggle.

Time-Management

The number of hours per day is given to each of us in equal measure – though you wouldn't think it when you see how 'rushed' some people are compared to others. **Decide that you're in charge of your time** – not that time is in charge of you! The following practical suggestions can help you master time.

1 **Work out the benefits to you of good time-management.** The benefits overlap with personal efficiency, productivity, and effectiveness. Well-developed time-management is a key to successful studying, and is central to avoiding all sorts of problems.

2 **Think in terms of 'learning payoff' when allocating time.** Some activities have a high learning payoff – including discussing, explaining things to others, summarizing, problem-solving, quizzing yourself, quizzing fellow-students. Other activities are low in learning payoff, (even though you may still have to do them), including 'passive' reading, writing essays, reports and practical work, and simply sitting in some classes!

3 **Stop and reflect on what you've just learned.** Look at what you've learned, how you learned it, and how you may be required in due course to *demonstrate* your learning. Stopping and reflecting is far better than just

21

'pressing on, hoping it's somehow going to stick'.

4   **Don't waste time thinking about starting work.**
    Highly intelligent people are capable of highly sophis-
    ticated *work-avoidance strategies!*

5   **Use the *first* 10% of the available time.** You've proba-
    bly noticed that left to human nature, 90% of most
    things gets done in the *last* 10% of the available time.
    Logically, that means it is perfectly feasible to do them
    just as well in the *first* 10% of the time. Think of all the
    other things you can then tackle in the remaining 90%
    of the time.

6   **Set your own deadlines** – don't rely on other people
    giving you them. Set stage deadlines as well as 'final'
    ones, breaking extended tasks into manageable
    chunks.

7   **Use the first half-hour to do something non-urgent.**
    Then get down to the main task. These half-hours
    soon begin to add up to a substantial investment of
    your time – and gradually you'll have fewer tasks
    becoming 'urgent' as you'll have already started
    them. (Planning to do half-an-hour of something non-
    urgent *after* finishing a task doesn't work!)

8   **Use the 'little bits' of time.** Even the busiest day has
    the odd-few-minutes of 'wasted' time here and there
    (before meals, between classes, on journeys, and so
    on). Use **some** of these short periods to do short but
    useful tasks (such as look back over a summary of a
    lecture, search for something you don't yet know,
    make a list of things to do by the end of the week, and
    so on).

9   **Tell other people about your time-management.**
    Knowing that someone is likely to ask you 'have you
    done what you said you would do?' is a strong incen-
    tive for making sure you can say 'yes'.

10 **Get ahead of schedule.** Try to deliberately work at

Tell other people about your time management.

least a couple of weeks ahead of where you need to be. This means that you won't be 'thrown' by the unexpected – illness, family problems, you name it! It's a great feeling when you've got 'time in hand' – and it helps your work to be even more productive when you're not wasting energy worrying about hand-in dates, assessment dates, and exam dates.

Getting Started on a Task

You've probably already found out that one of the hardest parts of any task is simply getting started. It seems to be human nature to put off the evil moment of starting – sometimes for weeks – even months. More daunting tasks are even easier to postpone! The suggestions on this page fall into two categories: avoiding not-starting – and making rapid headway once you do start. The suggestions can be applied to any major task – but particularly lend themselves to writing essays and reports.

1   First of all, **explore your work-avoidance strategies**. Look at the ones listed below, and take conscious steps to overcome any that apply to you.

Work-Avoidance Strategies to Avoid!

2   **Doing all sorts of 'tidying up', pretending you need to do so before starting work:** do the tidying up **after** working for half-an-hour or so. Then, your mind will still be processing the things you've been thinking about during your work.
3   **Doing easy little tasks, as a way of putting-off starting a big important one:** decide that you'll do half-an-

hour or so on the **big** task first, then spend a little time on the easy little tasks. You'll be surprised how much of a big task can get done in half-an-hour once you've started it.

4   **Finding 'displacement' activities:** it's all too easy to justify doing all sorts of other jobs rather than the one you know you should be doing. The remedy is simple – recognize displacement activities for what they are – work-avoidance strategies.

5   **Collecting together all the 'bits and pieces' you think you need before starting the task:** in fact this can just be another way of postponing the moment of really getting started on the task.

Ways of Really Getting Started

6   **Brainstorm 'what you know'.** On a blank sheet of paper put the key words from the task briefing in a little oval in the centre of the page, and draw 'spokes' one at a time radiating out from the oval, putting a word or two at the end of each spoke to record something you already know about the subject on which the task is based.

7   **Brainstorm 'what you don't yet know'.** Do this in the same way as '6' above, but this time putting **questions** at the end of the spokes, to create an agenda of the things you don't yet know about the task.

8   Decide which of the questions are the most crucial – and use your books and notes to find out answers – or use other people. Concentrate on things you **really need to know** to be able to do the task – ignore things that are in the 'nice to know' category

9   Combining the things you already know, and the things you've just found out, plan the most sensible

order of bringing them in to bear on the task. If it's an essay or a report, half-an-hour of planning can save hours in the long run.

10 **Start!** Once you've started, it's safe to have a break – or even do some displacement activities for a little while. A task started is well on its way to completion.

Maintaining Your Momentum

If you think back, you can probably pinpoint times in your life when you were learning efficiently, rapidly, and enjoyably. In other words, the momentum of your studies was high. You can also probably think of times when your momentum was 'sluggish' – and when you weren't enjoying your studies much at all. The suggestions below aim to help you to recapture at will those days of 'high momentum'.

1 **Get moving!** You can't maintain your momentum if you haven't got any. Even if you decide just to 'get moving' for the rest of this week, that's enough for a start. Then you can concentrate on maintaining your momentum using some of the suggestions below.
2 **Think of the benefits to you.** If your momentum is maintained, you have the benefit of greater confidence regarding success. But there's more – if your momentum is good, your efficiency is good too, which means you can get more done in less time – leaving more time for all the other things which you **enjoy** doing.
3 **Make plans – but 'flexible' plans.** The problem with 'rigid' study-plans is that sooner or later you 'fail' to meet them. This leaves you feeling stranded – maybe with 'no momentum'. Flexible plans are better – these

plans (for example) give you targets regarding what you're going to do by the end of the week, but without being too specific regarding 'which hours exactly' you'll be working.

4 **Keep consolidating what you've already done.** Don't hope that by magic all the things you learned last week will stay with you for the rest of your life. What you've already done is just as important as the things you're doing now, or the things still to come.

5 **Search for the 'cracks in your dam'.** If you suspect you have a weakness in material you've already covered, track it down. You don't have to 'rectify' it straight-away, simply knowing exactly where the problem lies is valuable.

6 **'Swim round obstacles'.** When you come to something new that you simply don't have a clue about, don't stop! Leave the obstacle behind like a little 'island'. The next topic you come to may be much more straightfor-ward, and the difficult topic may sort itself out when you've mastered a few more things.

7 **Don't exclude people.** Other people in your life (friends, partners, colleagues, relatives) can all help you maintain your momentum. They can do this best when they know about your hopes and plans.

8 **Build in holidays!** Don't pretend you'll work on Christmas day, for example. Plan to 'make up' for planned days-off **before** the holidays. You'll enjoy holi-days all the more when you feel you've 'earned' them in advance, and knowing that they're part of your plans.

9 **Plan your dose of 'flu, and Uncle Jack's funeral!** In other words, plan to **be ahead** sufficiently that when the unexpected comes up, you're able to handle it without losing your momentum. Being a week ahead is a nice feeling – being a month ahead is bliss! In such

circumstances, you can lie back and 'enjoy' your dose of 'flu – you'll recover all the quicker by not forcing yourself on.

10 **Be realistic.** Maintaining momentum is about being efficient – not superhuman. Choose a pace you can maintain as you build up your stamina. Accept that the 'fuel' for your momentum includes relaxation and recreation.

Experimenting with
Learning Styles

Much has been written about 'learning styles'. The subject
has acquired a jargon all of its own! Terms such as 'con-
crete experience', 'abstract conceptualization', 'reflective
observation' and 'active experimentation' are sometimes
used. However, most such discussions use the language of
educational psychologists – not very down to earth.
Below, you'll find six approaches to studying, followed by
some suggestions about how to use all of them – in every-
day plain English!

1   **Observe and question other people, then choose.** You
    can learn a lot from watching how other people tackle
    things – you can then choose which of several ways
    may be the best way for you to tackle it.
2   **Try various possibilities – then modify and improve
    approaches which are suitable for the task.** Trying
    various possibilities is better than sticking to the one
    you happen to know – even if that's the one which
    turns out to be most suitable for your task. There's just
    the chance that every now and then you stumble on
    a possibility which really works well for you – that
    otherwise you may not have discovered.
3   **Fix your direction, then concentrate your efforts.** For
    some kinds of study-task this method can be highly

recommendable. Having a firm target, and working steadfastly towards the target, ignoring all distractions, is suitable for tasks where determination and single-mindedness are sensible approaches.

4 **Repeat things that have succeeded for you – and avoid things that haven't.** Looking back to find out what has worked well for you in the past is always a useful approach. Applying techniques you're confident about helps you to develop trust in your approach. Similarly, consciously avoiding things that you know have proved risky in the past helps you avoid problems.

5 **Calculate your approach one step at a time, but remain flexible.** This has the benefits of making a careful choice about what is the best way to approach each task – plus the advantages of maintaining an open mind. This means when you realize that an alternative approach may be a good idea, you can adjust your plans accordingly.

6 **Play with ideas, then develop what turns up.** This is an 'open-minded' approach – rather like throwing everything up in the air and seeing what happens. This approach is the one where you may from time to time find out something completely new about ways of studying – and about yourself.

7 **Don't just stick with the one approach you happen to prefer.** Different tasks benefit from different approaches. Experimenting with the different approaches brings variety and interest to your study activities.

8 **Try a 'mixed-team' approach.** With two or three fellow students, decide that you'll tackle a particular task by each of you trying to apply a different approach to it. Then come together and compare your results. Your combined product as a team will be more interesting than the results of any of the individual approaches.

31

9   **When working on your own, try to apply at least two approaches simultaneously.** This helps to prevent you becoming 'blinkered' by too-narrow an approach. In any case, most tasks will be done better when you're approaching them in more than one way.

10   **Develop a learning-styles 'toolkit'.** The more you experiment with different approaches to learning, the better you can decide which techniques best suit any particular task in particular circumstances. Being able to 'pull the most productive style out of the bag for each different task' is a very useful skill to develop – it means you can adapt to new situations and circumstances quickly.

Facing up to Peaks and Troughs

Much as we may like the idea of being able to study efficiently on command, we're not machines or computers. We can't be plugged in or switched on and deliver exactly the expected performance at any time. The following suggestions can help you accommodate positive and negative extremes.

1   **Accept** that you'll have peaks and troughs. Don't regard any trough as 'too deep to climb out of'. It may feel 'deep' while you're in it, but once you're out of it, it looks a lot less significant. Mentally, develop your skill to take 'a helicopter view' of each situation – looking at it objectively as if from a height – and putting it into perspective.

2   **Capitalize on the peaks.** When you feel you're being particularly productive and efficient, forge ahead – make yourself 'spare time' for later. But don't forge ahead doing all sorts of irrelevant studying – even if you're tempted to. Use the 'peak' to get further ahead with things that are central to your studies.

3   **Break your workload down into manageable 'chunks'.** If you happen to be in a 'trough' there will still be some 'chunks' you can do perfectly satisfactorily – even though you're not feeling on top form. Use

the troughs to do some of the 'lower-level but necessary chunks' of work, saving more demanding tasks for when you're out of the trough.

4 **Be part of a group when you can.** Everyone has peaks and troughs – but if you're doing some of your studying as part of a learning syndicate, the syndicate itself will be more 'balanced' regarding peaks and troughs. Even just discussing your 'trough' with other people can make it seem a lot less serious.

5 **Don't hide your feelings from yourself.** There's a tendency for people to try to appear constant, steady and balanced at all times – stiff upper lip – and so on. While you may wish to hide some of your feelings from other people, it's useful to face up to your feelings yourself. It's all right to feel angry, frustrated, discouraged, 'down' – and elated, stimulated, 'fired', enthused.

6 **Use peaks and troughs as learning experiences.** During or after either extreme, spend a few minutes objectively analysing what you found out from the peaks or the troughs. There may be tangible outcomes that you can apply to help you make the most of your next peak – or to help you through your next trough.

7 **Get ahead of schedule.** Being ahead of schedule produces positive feelings – maybe contributing to 'peaks'. At the same time, when you're ahead of schedule, you're much less vulnerable to troughs – you've got time for them – and therefore probably won't get them anyway!

8 **If in a deep trough, don't be afraid to seek help.** 'A problem shared is a problem halved' has some merit as a proverb. Even the process of *putting your 'trough' into words* to explain it to someone else can help you to rationalize it and begin to climb out of it.

9 **Have several 'balls in the air' at once.** When there are

If in a deep trough, don't be afraid to seek help

several different things going on in your studies (and in your life as a whole), you can decide at any instant which 'ball' to work with. This means that you can make appropriate choices – even when in troughs or at peaks – there's always *something* you can be doing.

10 **Avoid transferring blame.** Indeed, a trough may not be your fault at all – it may be entirely someone else's fault – or it may be due to a combination of unfortunate circumstances you have no control over. But it doesn't help to think of 'fault' at all. The words 'if only . . . . .' are unproductive! Concentrate on what you *can do*.

Working in Groups

Your fellow-students can be the most powerful – and versatile – resource available to you. Sometimes you will be 'assigned' into groups for particular parts of your studies. However, there's no need to wait for such occasions – you can **choose** to form a group any time you wish – a 'home' group. The following suggestions can help you derive maximum benefit from your fellow students.

1   The benefits of becoming skilled in working with other people are **highly valued by employers** and will serve you well throughout your career. Now is your chance to develop skills such as teamwork, leadership – and the ability to be led.

2   Choose tasks for group work where **things are done better by a group** than by individuals working on their own. Such tasks include tracking down sources of information, planning written work, testing yourself, and brainstorming ideas.

3   **Avoid the feeling of competition.** The aim of working as part of a group should be that all members of the group benefit from cooperation. Remember for example that when you explain a topic to other members of a group, the person who does the most productive learning is *you*. Finding the words in which to

explain something is one of the best ways of coming to understand it.

4   **Avoid 'cheating'.** The purpose of working as part of a group should not be to make it possible for individuals to do less work. If all members of the group submit identical pieces of work for assessment, no-one is likely to gain credit or credibility. However, the group can *plan* a piece of work, then allow the members to prepare the final version in their own way.

5   **Establish some 'groundrules'.** These can lay down acceptable standards – for example punctuality, level of contribution to the group, and the constructive nature of critical comments.

6   Make the group **'task driven'.** Agree an 'agenda' for each meeting of the group, so that there is always a sense of purpose.

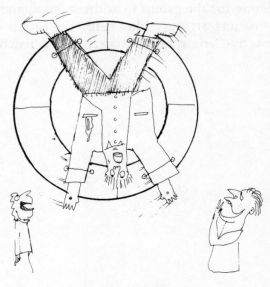

Rotate the leadership

7   **Rotate the leadership.** It's a good idea to have different 'leaders' for different tasks, so that all members of the group take on responsibility for particular aspects of the group's work.

8   **Share out 'chores'.** For example, share out the task of tracking down information, or collecting resources for a task. This can help make better use of the time of all members of the group, avoiding each member spending time chasing after identical books, papers and references.

9   **Make 'contracts' within the group.** Set deadlines for completing a task on behalf of the group. Make agreements regarding the different kinds of contribution to be made to the work of the group by each of its members.

10 **Maintain flexibility.** Even though the group will normally have an 'agenda', retain some time at each meeting for the group to address 'spontaneous' tasks or 'matters arising'. This helps the group develop a 'proactive' ethos, rather than simply a 'reactive' one.

Using your Lecturers

Your lecturers are expert witnesses in the various subject areas they represent. However, you may be able to get more from them than just lecture notes. The following suggestions point out some ways of making the most of your lecturers – good ones – and less good ones!

1 **Remember they're human!** Treating your tutors as fellow human beings is essential if you're hoping to

Remember they're human

39

maximize the benefit you can derive from them.

2 **Your lecturers are valuable sources of information.** They've probably been working in their respective subject areas for some years. Make it clear to them that you *value* their expertise.

3 **Your lecturers are sources of standards.** They know what 'counts'. They know what scores marks – and what loses marks. After all, many of them will also be your examiners in due course. When they see that you genuinely wish to prepare yourself to meet standards, they can provide a lot of help.

4 **Show interest.** When someone is obviously interested in their subject, most lecturers are only too pleased to spend a little extra time and energy explaining things, and giving pointers to further information.

5 **Avoid putting them 'on the spot'.** Lecturers (like anyone else) can feel vulnerable and intimidated if subjected to a barrage of questions – especially if 'instant replies' are expected. It is much better to hand lecturers lists of questions, saying 'can you have a look at these, and discuss them in a later class?' Alternatively, make appointments with your lecturers when you need something explained to you – but let them know what's involved before the appointments.

6 **Let them know who you are!** In large classes, it's hard for any lecturer to remember all the names and faces. Most lecturers *want* to be better at identifying members of their classes – remind them of your name when talking to them. Put your name on written questions you give them.

7 **Humour them!** Don't sit at the back and gaze out of the window. Don't fidget and yawn. Lecturers can become quite 'hostile' to people who seem to be threatening their work.

8 **Value the feedback your tutors give you.** When you

Let them know who you are!

receive back assessed coursework, take particular notice of any comments your tutors have written onto it. Where possible, discuss the work in more detail with them, aiming to find out as much as you can about how best to do similar work in the future. Don't be defensive about your work – being defensive quickly stems the flow of useful feedback.

9   **Be punctual.** Latecomers are noticed – it's not the sort of 'notice' that will do you any good. Similarly, when coursework is to be handed in by a given date, make sure yours is on time. Work which comes in late has usually been 'rushed' at the last minute – and is rarely high-quality work.

10 **Reward your lecturers' 'good behaviour'.** When tutors do things you like – let them know! Rather than grumble about what you don't like, find things you do like. When a tutor is thanked or congratulated for something, he or she will try to do more of it. By 'rewarding' good behaviour, you can 'train' your tutors to be better!

41

Using Other People

Besides your fellow students, there are many other people who can help you maximize your study potential – if you let them. The following suggestions may help you work out who can help you – and how.

1 **Use friends.** Don't ditch your friends because you're too busy studying to talk to them or write to them! Having friends who **know** what you're trying to do can be both a comfort and an incentive. Keep your friends informed. Let them know your targets and deadlines. Let them know your problems – you may well get some useful help from them.

2 **Use relatives.** There is a tendency either to take relatives for granted – or to exclude them from one's plans. However, when relatives feel that they can make a positive contribution to your studies, there's every chance they will prove really helpful. Involving relatives is good practice for you – and it helps your relatives understand the challenges and problems you face.

3 **Don't exclude people.** This particularly applies to close friends and partners. It's possible for such people to become resentful of the time you spend at your studies – and the consequent lack of attention to them! However, if you can build in ways in which they can

make positive contributions to your learning – for example by letting you learn by explaining things to them – they are likely to feel much less threatened by your studying.

4 **Get other people to quiz you.** It's highly likely that in due course you'll be measured on the basis of how well you can answer questions – for example: exam questions. While it's possible for you to quiz yourself, it's even better when someone else fires the questions at you. It's more like the real thing when you don't know exactly which question may come next. Also, other people can tell when you're 'waffling'!

5 **Use the expertise of library staff.** Librarians have considerable expertise and experience when it comes to tracking down relevant information. They often know a great deal about different sources of reference on a topic. They can sometimes arrange for computer-searches to identify a set of references on a topic. They

Use the expertise of library staff

are usually only too pleased to be able to help you – if you approach them in the right way.

6   **Remember there are Counsellors or Chaplains.** Hopefully, you won't need the services of these professional advisors. However, if you do need them – use them. They can provide invaluable help and backup. There's no harm talking to such people anyway – even when you've not got a problem. They are probably only to pleased to talk now and then to someone without a problem!

7   Be willing to learn from **other people's experiences and mistakes**. Getting to know some students on a later part of your course can be a useful move. They can often advise you on what could go wrong – and how best to avoid it.

8   **Accept advice** even when you decide not to use it. Make sure that people who offer you advice and help feel 'valued'. Where possible, give something back to those who help and advise you. Mutual help is the most productive and long-lasting.

9   **Don't forget Departmental Secretaries.** They may not know a great deal about your subject – but they probably know a lot about the people who do. A Departmental Secretary can often give you valuable suggestions about who to ask – and how to go about asking.

10 **Use the Students' Union.** It's not just a place to go to discos. Students' Unions offer help and advice on all manner of things, from finance to fitness.

Giving your Seminar

Giving a talk to your fellow students can be a daunting prospect – especially if you're doing it for the first time. The suggestions below will take much of the fear out of the prospect of giving your seminar, and help you to give a good one.

Preparing your Seminar

1 **Don't worry about it** – start doing something about it! The best way to soothe any anxiety you feel is to get going on something constructive. Start preparing your seminar as soon as you know what your topic is going to be.
2 **Prepare main points, a handout, and references to source materials.** The longer you spend preparing these components of your seminar, the more is your chance of 'polishing' them and improving them – leading to a high-quality seminar in due course.
3 **Prepare your visual support.** Overhead transparencies are simpler than slides. One advantage with an overhead projector is you can face your audience as you talk about your illustrations. A good overhead transparency has not too much on it – for example a list of

main points, a diagram or model. Use large lettering which can be read easily at the back of the room.

4   **Do some practice runs.** Time yourself, giving your seminar to an imaginary audience at first, then to a 'friendly' one. Get used to the sound of your own voice. The more often you've 'delivered' your seminar, the more naturally it will flow on the day.

On the Day . . . .

5   **Don't forget to introduce yourself – briefly. Explain what you're going to do – and how.** This makes your seminar seem a lot more logical and structured. When your audience knows how you're going to structure your seminar, they find it easier to follow your logic.

6   **Don't just read it out to your audience.** People don't like 'being read to'! When you're referring your audience to points on the screen (or points in your handout), talk *around* the words they can read for themselves. Have your own checklist of comments you're going to make – in large clear letters so you don't have to stoop to read your script.

7   **Involve your audience.** People quickly get bored if they're just watching and listening. Give them chances to participate. It can be as simple as '*how many of you have seen an example of* . . . . *?'* An important way of helping your audience to feel involved is to use **eye contact.** With a little practice, you can develop the ability to look at members of your audience without feeling anxious about it (even if you're just 'looking past' them!)

8   **Keep to time.** Watch the clock. There's nothing that irritates an audience more than someone who talks on and on. Even if keeping to time means missing out bits of your seminar, it's better to do this than to run late.

9 **Have 'extras' up your sleeve.** In the heat of the moment, you may talk a little faster than you did in your practice runs. Having one or two 'optional' parts to slip in to your seminar can spare you the embarrassment of finishing too early.

Have 'extras' up your sleeve

10 **Round it off well – don't just 'stop'.** A good seminar has a beginning, a middle – and an end. The 'end' tends to be the bit people really remember. It's sensible to give a sharp 'review' of the main points of your seminar at the end. Normally, this is followed by a time when you invite questions and comments from your audience – which is a clear signal that the main part of your seminar has been completed.

Using Open Learning Materials

The advantages of using open learning materials include working at your own pace, and at any time you choose, and wherever you want. Open learning materials require you to work **actively** – they're not meant just to be read. The following suggestions can help you get the most from your open learning materials.

1   Check whether there are things you should already be able to do before you start working through the open learning materials. Information such as 'prerequisites' is often given at the start.

2   If the material gives **objectives** one way or another, pay particular attention to these and keep returning to see how well you are getting on towards mastering them. Objectives are usually phrased along the lines 'when you've completed this package, you should be able to . . . .'

3   Most open learning materials (good ones) are 'active' and contain things for you to do as you work through them. These active parts are sometimes called **self-assessment questions** or **activities**. However tempted you are to skip these and read on, don't skip them! Even if you think you know the answer, jot it down, **then** compare what you did with the answer or

response given in the material.

4 When you get a question right, be pleased with yourself. When you get one wrong, be even more pleased – you've found out something useful. Find out exactly **why** you didn't get the right answer – and remember this for next time.

5 When you come to a bit that has you stumped, don't struggle with it for ages. Skim ahead and see what's coming next. The next bit may be straightforward. Make a note of exactly what you don't understand about the bit that stumped you, and plan to find out from someone how to deal with that bit. It's probably quite simple when you've got someone who can explain it to you – even though you may never have worked it out on your own.

6 Open learning materials often contain a great deal of information – don't try to learn it all as you proceed. Make decisions about what is required to be learned, as opposed to the things you are merely required to understand as you read them. It's very useful to work with fellow students for this – you'll all have slightly different views about exactly what is important and what isn't – the truth will be closer to the average than to one person's view.

7 If you've been given your own copy of the open learning material, make it **belong** to you, by writing your own comments and notes all over it (as well as by writing in the answers to questions and activities). You'll often remember the things you added to the material – a useful way of boosting what you remember about the topics involved.

8 Keep looking back – remind yourself of the things you've already done. The more often these things have been through your mind the more firmly you'll understand them.

9 Keep glancing ahead to see what's coming next. You'll often understand **why** you're doing something only when you see where it's leading towards.

10 Have another go at all the self-assessment questions and activities – again and again where they are difficult. Your ability to do something difficult depends more on how often you've tried doing it than on how thoroughly you did it once.

Overcoming Problems

Every now and then you can expect problems! There are all sorts of problems – personal ones, study ones, 'people' ones – you name it! Some would say you're not alive if you haven't got a problem or two! There's nothing wrong with having problems. The following suggestions can help you turn problems to your advantage – every problem solved is an achievement for you.

1   **Accept that you may have a problem.** Don't look for a miracle or an 'instant' solution. Don't waste time transferring the blame – even if it's not your fault! 'Blame allocation' doesn't help towards solving problems. A problem is only a problem if you have no idea how to solve it – once you've worked out a course of action, the problem becomes a challenge – an opportunity for you to solve it.

2   Work out exactly **what the problem is.** It's all too easy to feel that the whole world is conspiring against you – but when you start being objective about it, it's usually the case that only a few things are really getting you down – or perhaps just one problem.

3   Decide **who the problem really belongs to.** Sounds obvious – but many people spend a lot of time worrying about other people's problems. Sometimes there's

51

not a lot you can do about other people's problems – the only ones you can really try to solve are **yours** – so find out whether you own a problem before spending a lot of energy trying to solve it.

4 **Talk about your problem to someone** – several people if possible. Just the fact of putting your problem into words often makes it seem less serious – and more manageable. Choose carefully who you wish to bring into your confidence. For some problems, it's wise to talk to someone you don't know too well – even someone you may never wish to talk to again once you're over the problem.

5 **Work out why the problem arose.** This may not help you solve the present problem, but it may help you avoid similar problems arising again. Remember that you're extremely unlikely to have invented a brand new problem all by yourself. Try to find out how other people developed similar problems – and how they reacted to them.

6 **Work out how you could make the problem worse.** (Don't make it worse!) Actions which would make the problem worse can often be the *reverse* of things that will help to overcome the problem. Besides, it's sometimes reassuring to speculate just how much worse things could have been!

7 **Decide three ways of improving the situation.** One something you can do at once, one something you can do in the immediate future, and one longer-term action you can plan.

8 **Tell someone what you're planning to do.** If your actions are difficult, it's very valuable to have someone who knows you're trying hard to do something – and it helps you to make sure that you do indeed try to do something about the problem straightaway – rather than continue to postpone actions.

9   **Keep a log of what you do.** This helps you to feel that
    you are tackling the problem in a structured and
    organized way, and making progress – even if it's
    slow progress.

10 **Regard each problem as an opportunity to grow.**
    Even the most painful problem can turn out to be a
    valuable learning experience. People who overcome
    many problems develop valuable skills and self-
    reliance which serves them well in many aspects of
    their lives and careers – including the ability not to
    give in.

Notemaking versus Notetaking

The notes you make in lectures and other group sessions are one of the most important resources you build up during your studies. However, many people only get as far as notetaking – not **notemaking**. The suggestions below point towards several ways you can turn notemaking into a valuable start in the business of getting to grips with your subject material.

1 **Don't just copy**. Don't just write down what you see on the screen or blackboard, or what you hear. It's too easy to copy things down without thinking about them in any depth. Put things into your own words, in your own way. Don't write long, full sentences when you can summarize them in a few well-chosen words. The process of **deciding** exactly what you're writing keeps your mind alert – and helps prevent boredom.

2 **Experiment with layout**. Make every page of your notes look different. This helps make every page more memorable. Don't fill all of the paper – leave space for later additions and amendments.

3 **Take your own decision** regarding when to write something down. Don't just write when everyone around you starts to write. Don't worry if you're the only one writing – others will probably soon imitate

you! Make notes whenever you feel something is worth capturing.

4   Ask yourself **'what am I expected to become able to do?'** all the time. Make your notes so that they remind you of what may be expected of you – and so that they help you become able to meet expectations. Be receptive to all clues regarding the sort of thing you may be asked to do in due course. Don't bank on remembering these clues – write them down.

5   **Make important things stand out** in your notes. Make each page so that a glance tells you what the main ideas and concepts are. Use colour, boxes, highlighters, patterns, and any other ways you know to make the important things stand out from the background detail. **Capture the emphasis** given away by tone of voice, facial expression, and repetition. Make your notes reflect all such emphasis. Tone of voice and such things are quickly forgotten, but you can capture your interpretation of them in the way you make the important things in your notes stand out on each page.

6   **Don't switch off** when you've got a handout. Add things to the handout all the time, making it **yours.** Use the occasion to help you turn the information on the handout into something much more than the original handout. (If you're expecting to be given a handout later, don't take anything for granted – make notes! The handout may miss important things).

7   Write in **your own questions** every time there's something you don't yet understand. Also write in **your own reactions and comments**. Your notes then become a record of your thinking – not just a transcript of things someone said.

8   **Compare your notes,** when possible with those of two or three other people. Add in ideas you missed. Put right things you noted down wrongly.

9 **Work through your notes again** within a day or two –
before you've forgotten the meaning of questions and
cryptic coded comments you may have written into
them. Continue to work on your notes regularly,
adding further things into them, correcting things,
explaining things, and linking with other sources of
material.

10 Turn each set of notes into **lists of questions** (reflecting all the things you may be asked to be able to do
with the material concerned) and **summaries** (containing all the important 'bare bones' of each topic).
Practise with the questions, using the summaries as
prompts.

Developing your Speed Reading

Speed reading can be a valuable skill, enabling you to cover much more subject material than you may have thought. Of course, speed reading has its limitations – it serves little purpose in many mathematical or scientific materials where the subjects are unfolded step by step – but is still useful for the more descriptive parts of such subjects. Also, when reading for pleasure you may be quite content to read at your own 'natural' speed. Speed reading for learning should be done in short, purposeful bursts rather than sustained periods.

1 **Use the contents pages** to get a rapid picture of what a book contains, especially the first time you use the book. Make notes of the chapters or sections which seem to be most relevant to your studies.
2 Decide **when** speed reading is going to be appropriate. For example, if your purpose is to gain a rapid perspective of a subject, speed reading can help. If, however, you need to find out detailed information, speed reading is only helpful in tracking down the portions of a book you need to study in depth.
3 **Test out whether speed reading actually works** on the book you're studying. Some books lend themselves to speed reading (for example when there are

numerous headings and subheadings, and when the first sentence of any paragraph gives you a lot of information about what's contained in the rest of the paragraph).

4 Try speed reading by skimming through headings and subheadings, first and last sentences of paragraphs, and the whole of first and last paragraphs of sections or chapters.

5 Try to **break any habit** you may have of reading at the speed that you would 'speak' the words. Most of us learned to read by following words at spoken speed – in fact our brains can handle words much faster than we can speak them. Yet many readers never really start reading faster than they can 'vocalize'.

6 Practise taking in **clusters of words**, rather than every single word. In most phrases, only one or two words are fundamental – the others need not be 'read' to gather the meaning of the phrase.

7 As you develop your skills at speed reading, **make an 'agenda'** before you start to read. For example, write down a list of questions you wish to find answers to. Then, as you speed-read, your mind automatically tends to store the information which answers the questions you've prepared.

8 When you already know a fair amount about a subject, spend a few minutes **listing key points** you already know before starting to speed-read. This helps your speed reading 'top up' your existing knowledge, allowing you to skim faster through things you already know. There's no point spending time reading things you already know.

9 **Keep glancing back.** Keep turning a few pages back, and reminding yourself of the main points you've learned as you've been speed reading. Also check whether you find anything important 'new' each time

you glance back – it's possible to miss important things the first time you speed-read something.

10 **Keep glancing ahead,** unless you're reading fiction, as well as back. Knowing what's coming next is often useful in tuning your mind in to what you're reading. What's coming next may give you clues about **why** things are arranged in the order they're written.

Active Reading

You've heard the expression 'reading for a degree'? It's rather misleading. Now if it were 'writing for a degree' perhaps it would be nearer the truth. However, reading is something you'll do a lot of in your studies. The suggestions below should help you make your reading more efficient – and should help you avoid some of the dangers which can be associated with reading – and I don't mean eyestrain.

1 **Put reading into perspective.** When you read something, how much of it do you actually remember – say two weeks later? 50%? 10%? 5%? If you're honest with yourself, you'll admit that 'just reading' isn't a very efficient way of studying. Reading has to be made 'active' in one way or another.

2 **'Further Reading . . .':** how often these words come up! Is it assumed that you will go off and read **all** of the books and references suggested to you for 'further reading'? By definition, **further** reading is not **'central'** reading – it's the additional icing on the cake. If you spend all your time doing 'further reading' you'll be away at a tangent to the fundamental things you're meant to be studying – these are often in your own notes or in 'central' books and papers.

3   **Find the really relevant parts – before you get side-tracked.** The most useful pages of many books are the **'Contents'** pages – and the **index**. Use these to track down exactly where the most relevant part of the book is.

4   **Make an 'agenda' before you start reading.** Work out what you need to pick up from each source you use – write some questions you need answers for. Then, as you read, when you come across the answers to your questions, the answers will 'register' – because the questions were in your mind already. Without an agenda, you'd simply skim right over much of the most valuable information.

5   **If the book belongs to you – make it 'your own'.** Write notes on the pages, use a highlighter pen to make the really important parts easy to find again. This allows you to progressively consolidate your work with the book – every time you see things you've already done to the book you're reminded of thinking you've already done. (But don't do any of this to library books – make photocopies first.)

6   **Write questions as you read.** When you've just learned something important, jot down a question which will give you the chance to test yourself on it later (with a page reference for when you need to have another look at the book). Build lists of such questions as you go. **Active** reading is done with a pen!

7   **Summarize as you read.** Make notes of the things you think you **really** need to remember (probably quite a small percentage of the average page). Put page references on your summary points, then a few days later look at your summary and try to mentally reconstruct some of the content of the book – going back to the pages where something has slipped your mind. **Active** reading is done with a pen – again!

8 **Prioritize your reading list.** This becomes possible as you get to know your books and references rather better. Divide the books and references into categories such as 'essential and useful', 'useful for some things', 'has a very useful chapter 5 – ignore the rest' and so on. Then spend most of your reading time with the books with 'high learning payoff' – relevant, useful ones.

9 **Balance your reading** with all the other study-tasks on your agenda. Don't spend too much time reading – remember it's still not the most efficient way of learning.

10 **Read for pleasure too** – but as a reward after doing some useful work – not as a way of putting off the task of starting some real work!

Assessed Coursework

Even if the main part of your assessment is through exams, you're likely to have assessed coursework as well. Assessed coursework can be very useful in helping you to find out more about exactly what standards you're aiming for. The following suggestions can help you get the most from your assessed coursework as part of a logical strategy to succeed overall.

1 **Find out how much your assessed coursework is worth.** If it's worth 50% of your overall score or grade for a course, it's logical to spend about 50% of your time and energy on it. If it's worth much less, take care not to give it a disproportionate amount of time and energy – prepare for the things that count most.
2 **Start early – straightaway if possible** when given some assessed coursework. That gives your mind longer to get to grips with the subject matter concerned, leaving plenty of time for second thoughts.
3 **Work out what's really wanted.** If the assessed work is a set of calculations or problems this is straightforward enough. However, if you have an essay title or a project, there may be several ways of tackling the task ahead. Discuss with other people their view of what's likely to be expected.

4   **Work out likely criteria** by which the work may be assessed. If you can make an informed guess at the assessment criteria, you can tailor your answers to live up to as many of these criteria as you can. When working out criteria, it's useful to do so with a few other people who are addressing the same question.

5   Make sure that you are **really answering the question** as you proceed to address each task. It's all too easy to wander off on tangents – these score few (if any) marks – and may irritate the person who assesses your work. Build words and phrases into your answers which remind the reader of the specific parts of the task you are addressing.

6   Pay particular attention to the **first things** your assessor will read. The introduction to a piece of work sets up an impression – you want this to be a good impression. It's often sensible to write the introductory parts only **after** drafting the rest of the work, so you know exactly what you're leading up to.

7   **Make conclusions or answers stand out clearly.** Check that these are exactly what the question or task asked you to do. For example if the question said 'decide' make sure a clear decision is evident in your conclusions.

8   **Keep a copy of the question** before you hand in the work for assessment. Assessed coursework can be a 'dry run' for a future exam question – it's useful to put in some further practice with the question from time to time.

9   **Hand your answers in on time** – or early. Punctual coursework is much appreciated by assessors. The best answers are seldom ones which come in late. Even if you know the work is poor – hand it in anyway – you'll get some marks – more than the **zero** you'd get if you didn't hand it in at all!

10 When you get your work back, get as much as you
    can from any **comments** which are written onto it.
    Don't be preoccupied with your score or grade. From
    the comments your assessor has written, you can pick
    up a lot of information about how the examiner's
    mind may work, or find out more about how to make
    your next piece of assessed coursework produce a
    good grade or score.

Summarizing

Summarizing is an extremely useful skill – and is developed by practice. Being skilled at summarizing helps you reduce the amount you need to learn to manageable proportions. Summarizing automatically gets you **making decisions** about what is important and what is not. Summarizing helps you to avoid the wasted time and energy which can go into mere 'passive reading'.

1 **Consciously decide to reduce** the amount of information you need to learn. When working with textbooks in particular, aim at 'extracting' the important things from the book into something that you can use in future instead of the book.

2 Plan to become able to **work from your summaries** progressively, rather than from original notes and references. It can take far less time to re-read a summary than going through several pages of original material – yet the amount of **thinking** you do while working with a summary can be just as great. Make your summaries cover all the main concepts and ideas which you may be expected to master.

3 Looking at a page of your notes (or a page of a book), decide **which three things** are most important on that page – i.e. which would you be most likely to be

required to know. Jot down the three things in as concise a way as possible – aim for one-line phrases or sentences.

4   Make **diagram** summaries. For example, while reading books or revising your notes, draw an oval in the middle of a card or a small sheet of paper. Write in the oval a topic or question. Draw 'spokes' radiating out from the oval, adding one or two words at the end of each spoke – just enough to remind you of important aspects or facts concerning the topic.

5   Using a diagram as above, or starting with a list of points about a subject, **prioritize them.** Decide what the most important point is first, then the next-most-important – and so on. A good summary should only contain important points – getting rid of the less-important points is a useful step towards making effective summaries.

6   Make **portable** summaries – allowing you to use them anywhere and everywhere. A small pocket book is one approach. Alternatively, use small filing-cards. Index the summaries clearly, so you can quickly track down a particular summary.

7   Practise using your summaries to help you **reconstruct** some of the fine detail about the topics concerned. Check with your original material to see what you missed, then add a few words to your summary to ensure that you'll be prompted to recall it successfully next time.

8   **Compare your summaries with other people's.** If several of you make summaries, naturally they'll all be different – added together they may be extremely useful. Try to work out whose summary would prove most useful – and learn from other people's ways of going about the task of summarizing. Try out as many ways as you can find.

9 When ending an essay or report with a summary, remember that this will be the **last thing** that is read by your assessor – maybe seconds before deciding your mark or grade! Therefore, take care with such summaries – make them high in quality.

10 When writing summaries of essays or reports, make sure that your summary **addresses the title or question** you started out with. Don't repeat lots of material from the main part of your writing – just repeat the most important conclusions.

Using Questions

'If only I'd known what the questions were going to be' is a common lament after exams. With a little planning, you can work out what **all** the questions could be – by building up your own personal **question bank.** This could be in a pocket book or on filing cards. You may also add 'clues' on the reverse of the pages or cards, to give your memory that extra 'nudge' when needed. The suggestions below should help you track down material for your question bank – and put it to good use.

1 **Make your own question bank.** Looking at a page of your notes (or a book) ask yourself 'what am I reasonably expected to be able to **do** with this?' Then turn what you could be asked about it into *short, sharp questions – lots of them.* If you build a question bank all the way through your studies, you'll be able to answer *any reasonable question* – not just the ones that happen to turn up in your exam.

2 Collect and store questions from **worked examples** or **case studies** done in class. Separate the questions or tasks from the answers. This means you practise on the questions without robbing yourself of the chance to think (if the answer is in sight – eyes stray!).

3 Collect and store questions from **homework** or

assignments. Such questions are often 'dry runs' for the sort of question you'll get in an exam. Separate the questions from your solutions or assignments, so that you can practise with the questions without being prompted by your earlier work.

4   Collect and store **old exam questions**. You can usually arrange to buy old exam papers. It's better to get hold of these **early** – don't worry that you won't be able to answer them yet! In fact, it's very useful to have such questions in the back of your mind *before* you cover a topic – it makes you more receptive to the information which will enable you to answer such questions.

5   Use **clues** and **hints** from your tutors. In class, you'll often get the feeling that something is being 'plugged' rather hard – this could be a clue that it's important. Tone of voice, facial expression, and repetition can all give pointers to things worth paying particular attention to. Turn the clues and hints into **questions** so you can practise.

6   Use **problems and exercises** from relevant textbooks – particularly worked examples (taking care not to scan the solutions). Select relevant tasks and add them to your question bank (with a reference to remind you where you can find the solution).

7   **Work with fellow students on formulating questions.** If three of you sit down for five minutes and each write '10 important questions', then share, you'll soon have more than the ten you thought of yourself. Add them to your question bank.

8   **Practise with your question bank.** You can practise in minutes – as well as for longer periods of time. It only takes minutes to scan 20 questions and find out which ones you **can't yet answer**. It's very useful to find such questions. You can then plan ways of getting to grips with them.

70

9 **Get people to quiz you.** When someone else fires questions at you, you're less able to kid yourself along the lines 'oh, I really know how to answer that, but . . . .'. When possible, work with fellow students, quizzing each other and judging each other's answers.

10 Exams measure how **practised** you are at **answering questions.** Spend part of each study session (right from day 1) practising with some of the questions you should be able to answer.

Problem Solving

Your ability to solve problems is best developed by practising solving problems. Seems obvious, doesn't it? Your
skills at problem solving depend more on how many problems you've solved than on how much knowledge you've
got at your disposal to solve the problems with.

1   When faced with **a problem you have not addressed
    before**, spend a few minutes brainstorming solutions
    as follows: jot down the gist of the problem in a little
    oval in the middle of a blank sheet of paper, and draw
    'spokes' radiating in all directions – one at a time –
    jotting an idea that may be useful in solving the prob-
    lem at the end of each spoke. Then look back and
    decide which ideas are the most sensible ones to start
    with.

2   **If the problem is a 'difficulty'** it's sometimes worth
    trying a 'negative brainstorm'. Do this the same way as
    '1' above, but this time jot down all sorts of things that
    would make the problem *worse*. Then look to see which
    of these negative ideas can be turned backwards to
    lead to positive contributions to solving the difficulty.

3   **Create a 'problem bank'**. Collect together (in a pocket
    book or on cards) all the problems you have solved (in
    lectures, homework, tutorials, etc) but *without* their

72

solutions. Jot down where the solution is to be found. Then practise regularly with the problems without looking at the solutions except for checking.

4   **Turn problems you have solved into variants**. Alter conditions and numbers. Practise solving the different forms of these problems. (Different forms of problems you've already solved often come up as exam questions).

5   **Extract problems from old exam papers** and add them to your problem bank. Add to your problem bank problems extracted from worked examples and case studies in textbooks. Practise frequently with your problem bank.

6   **Practise 'skeleton' problem solving sometimes**. Don't write full answers, just jot down the key stages or operations involved in solving the problems. This way, you can get through many more times the problem-solving activity than you would have done if you'd solved the problems in full written answers.

7   **Create problems of your own** as you work through notes and handouts. Keep asking yourself 'what sort of problems will this information help me to solve?' and write problems along these lines.

8   Join with two or three fellow students and form a **problem syndicate**. Set each other problems, then assess each others' answers as though you were examiners.

9   Note how the more **frequently** you solve particular kinds of problems, the **faster** you get at solving them. This can mean that in an exam you can tackle similar problems with the knowledge that you'll be able to do them in less than the normal time-per-question – saving time for other questions.

10 Whenever you can't solve a particular problem, **get help from someone who can**. Then look back and

make a note of exactly which step eluded you. Once you know what the cause of the block is, the block doesn't occur again.

Improving Your Memory

Ever thought your memory isn't as good as it used to be? Do you face situations (for example, some kinds of exam) where a good memory is important – or at least useful? Read on for some ideas to improve your use of your memory.

1 **Convince yourself that your memory is good**. Think back to yesterday. Think of the main meal you ate yesterday. Imagine you had several sheets of paper to write down things you remembered about that meal – the food, what it tasted like, what it looked like, who else was there, where you were, what you said, what you thought – and on and on. All this information that you *don't* need is stored there. You can store information you do need just as efficiently.

2 In a pocket book **make a list of things you forget**. It's useful to find out exactly what sort of things you're likely to forget – you can then focus on not forgetting them again. The real problem is not knowing what you've forgotten – tackle that problem.

3 If you've got numbers to remember, **make little sentences that can help you reconstruct the numbers** – choose words with the same number of letters in them as the numbers. For example:

4 **Turn the things you may forget into questions**, and spend a few minutes each day practising answering the questions – noting those where you still keep forgetting the answer.

5 **Get other people to quiz you** on the questions where you're likely to forget the answers. It doesn't matter who – you will know when you're answering the questions well – and when you're making the answers up!

6 **Make lists on cards** of facts and figures you need to remember. Spend a few minutes each day practising reproducing each list, noting which items you remember and which you've forgotten. Make new lists of things you keep forgetting and practise with them. Be pleased every time you find out something you've forgotten. Once you know what you've forgotten you can do something about it. The more often you've forgotten something important, the less likely you are to forget it again. Memory depends more on how often you've remembered something, not on how firmly it was in your mind on one particular occasion.

7 **Find out exactly what you need to remember**. Use old exam questions (and coursework questions) to make lists of those points you would need at your fingertips to be able to answer the questions successfully and quickly.

8 Work out what you **don't** need to remember. People waste a lot of time learning things they couldn't reasonably be expected to remember. Keep asking yourself 'do I have to remember this, or simply become able to use it when given it?'

9 **Work with fellow students**, quizzing them on things you may all need to remember. This is useful for

finding out how your memory compares with theirs. Keep at it till you're satisfied that you're doing as well or better than other people.

10 **Don't clutter your mind with unnecessary things**. Make lists of things you've got to do and tick them off as you do them. This gives a feeling of satisfaction as you cross things off your lists.

Increasing Your Motivation

Ask any group of new students to answer the simple question 'why are you here?' and you'll get a surprisingly diverse range of replies. When you're enjoying every minute of your studies there's no problem – you don't even need motivation then. However when you come to a tough patch, without some solid motivation it can be only too easy to surrender and give up. You may know very well what needs doing – and how to do it – but without motivation you could be lost. The following analysis of various kinds of motivation may help you find good reasons of your own for staying with your studies.

1   **Make a list of reasons why you want to succeed.** Ask yourself 'what's in it for me?' and write down as many things as you can think of. Add to your list any other reasons why it's important for you to be successful in your studies. Then compare your own list with the suggestions and comments given below.
2   **Your own reasons** are the most important ones. You may well have on your list some reasons for studying which reflect other people's expectations of you – but in the final analysis you need reasons of your own to see you through the difficult days. While it's natural to want to live up to other people's expectations, don't

make these your only driving force.

3   **'Because I enjoy the subject'** is a useful reason for studying it. However, don't make this your only reason for learning it – your enjoyment could change to frustration when you come across more difficult areas of the subject later. All subjects have their 'unenjoyable' parts sooner or later.

4   **'Because I want to prove I can do it'** is a useful motivator. It seems to be a powerful one too – most people succeed in doing anything they really want to do.

5   **'Because I had the right entry qualifications':** this is a rather lame motivator. Of course, it's useful to have a good starting position, but this won't help you unless you've also got good reasons for moving ahead. Sadly, some students 'drift' into higher education just because their exam results provided passports – but they don't really know why they're there.

6   **'Because so-and-so did it':** many students seem to be following in the footsteps of brothers or sisters or parents. This is fair enough as long as they have some good reasons of their own for studying.

7   **'Because I want to be a social anthropologist'** (substitute **your** career-dream): it's useful to have an idea of where you're heading. This is likely to be a motivator which belongs to **you** rather than anyone else, and is the sort of thing that may keep you going in the difficult days.

8   **'Because I want to maximize my choices in life':** this is one of the best motivators. If you come to regard success at your studies as having a strong influence on the breadth of career choices available to you, it gives you both a sense of real purpose – and a flexible approach to new choices as they become available to you.

9   **'Because I want to find my feet in the world before settling down':** many students regard higher

education as an opportunity for freedom. The danger is that this view can be counter-productive to successful studying. If you resolve to make your studying both purposeful and efficient, you can make yourself time to exploit your freedom – rather than enjoy freedom at the expense of your studies.

10 **Keep your motivation in view.** When you've worked out what your own real reasons for studying are, pin them up somewhere where you can see them often. On those days when nothing seems worthwhile, remind yourself of all the benefits to you of sticking at it.

Getting at Assessment Criteria

If you knew in advance exactly what was required by assessors of your coursework and exams, you'd be able to prepare to give it to them – **you can do this!** For coursework and exams, there are usually definite criteria used by assessors. There's usually a 'marking scheme' showing exactly how many marks are to be awarded for each part of a good answer – and how many are to be lost for each probable mistake. These marking schemes are required by external examiners and moderators so that the fairness of assessment can be monitored. Sadly, most tutors keep their marking schemes to themselves! However, you can get very close to a marking scheme if you follow the suggestions below – especially if you collaborate with fellow students in your efforts to find out how examiners' minds work.

1 **Get hold of old exam papers.** You can usually purchase these. Old papers don't exactly tell you what the assessment criteria may be, but they provide abundant clues to help you work them out for yourself.
2 **Use feedback from tutors on marked coursework.** If your score or grade is low – don't bin the work in a fit of pique. Do some detective work on the marked work – try to find out how the examiners' minds may work.

Look for occasions when you lost marks – and look for the ways you did actually score marks. All this helps you to pinpoint the assessment criteria you're working to meet.

3 If your syllabus is written in the form of **aims** and **objectives**, take special note of these. The assessment criteria will be closely tied to the objectives. Practise achieving the objectives. Look at coursework and exam questions to see which objectives they relate to.

4 Keep asking yourself **'what could I reasonably be expected to become able to do with this?'** – for every task you do, for every page of your notes – for everything. Often, the answer will be 'not a lot!' – these are bits you need not spend much time learning. When there are firm answers to the question, make sure you become **practised** at doing whatever it is.

5 Looking through the material you've already covered, **write out a selection of possible exam questions**. You may be able to ask your tutors whether your questions are a reasonable reflection of the *standard* of the exam. (Don't ask 'are these questions coming up?'!)

6 Be alert to **clues and hints**. Tutors often make helpful suggestions when they set coursework tasks.

7 **Work with fellow students when you can.** For example, if a group of students looks at an old exam question, it's possible in a few minutes to 'brainstorm' ways of tackling the question. You may learn more from this few minutes than if you'd spent half an hour working on the question by yourself.

8 **Try to work out the criteria for yourself.** When you're set coursework, ask yourself 'what could they be looking for here? What will count in a good answer?'

9 **Look carefully at the structure and wording of each question and task.** If the question is in three parts, there will be marks for each part – you may be able to

make a sensible guess about which part carries most marks.

10 Brainstorm **'mark-scoring points'** for questions and tasks. (This is even more productive when done with some fellow students). Jot down rapidly a word or two about anything that might score marks. Then look back and decide which are the most important mark-scoring points, and which are the 'luxury' ones, or 'marginal' ones.

Using Your Syllabus

There seems to be a tendency for some tutors to keep the syllabus 'their secret'! Remember, **you** have to learn it! Get hold of the detail of your syllabus as soon as you can (even before your course starts if possible). The following suggestions show how you can use your knowledge of the syllabus to structure your learning productively.

1 **Use it to find out where you're at.** Your syllabus helps you find out exactly where you are in the context of the whole of your course. It's useful to know what's coming next – and how much more in total you've got to cover.

2 **Use it as a guide to what you're expected to become able to do.** Sometimes a syllabus is written in terms of objectives or competence statements – either of these describes 'learning outcomes' which are a very convenient way for you to find out exactly what standard you're aiming to meet.

3 **Looking at the whole syllabus helps you select the most useful books.** Use your syllabus to help you find books which cover *most* of the things you're going to cover.

4 **Comparing one syllabus with another** helps you to see the connections and overlaps between one subject

and another. This often helps you find out why particular topics are important.

5   Your syllabus may help you find out **what you're
    expected to be able to do already**. A syllabus often
    describes 'prerequisite knowledge and skills' – in other
    words the things you're assumed to have mastered
    before you start.

6   **Pick on bits of the syllabus you've not yet covered**
    and brainstorm what you already know about it.

7   Use your syllabus to find things you're about to cover,
    **brainstorm questions about the topics which are
    coming up**. This makes you more receptive to the
    answers to the questions as they unfold.

8   **Select parts to cover on your own.** Set yourself
    'research projects' and try to find out as much about
    some topics as you can.

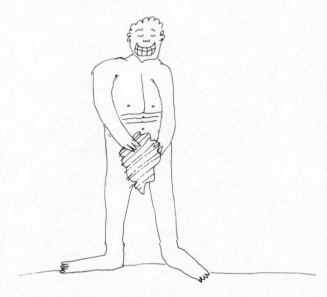

Select parts to cover on your own

9 **Compare your syllabus to past exam papers.** Look carefully at the different ways topics on the syllabus are tested. Use the exam papers to make importance-judgements about the various topics on your syllabus.
10 **Get started on topics on your syllabus which may be covered 'late' in your course.** This helps you avoid the danger of having too little time to really get to grips with these topics.

Writing Essays

In many subjects, much of your assessment depends not only on how much you know, but also on how well you can put it across in writing. The following suggestions present a logical sequence for preparing and writing essays.

1   **Get started straightaway.** This gives you longer to reflect on your ideas, and far more opportunity to refine and polish your essay in due course.
2   **Don't start by writing the introduction.** It's best to do the introduction later, when you know exactly what you're leading up to. An introduction which 'isn't lived up to' tends to lose marks!
3   **Brainstorm.** Brainstorm things you already know about the topic, and also brainstorm things you don't yet know (questions and issues) that you may need to find out. Just write key words at this stage, not whole sentences.
4   **Look carefully at the question or title,** and give 'relevance ratings' to the various ideas you've brainstormed. For example, give *** to key ideas, ** to fairly important ones, * to background points. Anything that doesn't get any *s can be safely missed out.
5   **Decide the most logical sequence.** Look again at your various possibilities, and decide which is the most

sensible starting point. Then look for where to lead next, and so on.

6 **Start putting the middle together.** Pick on ideas or arguments that are going to be in the middle of the essay, and turn each into a short paragraph (on separate bits of paper – or on your word processor). Since most of the essay consists of the 'middle', now's the time to check that you're going to be within 20% or so of any **word limit** that may have been set.

7 **Write the ending** – after you've got most of the 'middle' drafted. Then you can ensure that the ending really does sum up the content of the essay. Make sure that the ending is carefully related to the exact wording of the question or title.

8 **Start your editing.** Each paragraph should be about a single complete issue or point. It's best if it's possible to tell what the paragraph is going to be about just by reading the first sentence. People (including assessors and examiners) often read just the first sentences of each paragraph to get a feeling of the content of an essay.

9 **Write the introduction** – when you know exactly what the essay did, and how it was done, and what the conclusions were! Write an introduction which points towards what you've done – it will then be 'lived up to' automatically.

10 **'Drawer-it'!** Before writing (or printing) your final version, leave it alone for some days, then return to it. Re-read it with 'fresh eyes'. This helps you find out what sort of first impression it may make on other readers. You'll also be able to make corrections and amendments.

Writing up Practical Work

Practical work is 'learning by doing' – but don't forget that exam questions can cover things you do as part of practical sessions. Many exam questions ask you to analyse and interpret data in the same way as you've done with the results of your practical sessions.

1 Where possible, **prepare for practical work.** Go carefully through any printed instructions. Check up on the background to the practical work. Work out what it's there for. Check through the theory upon which it may be based.

2 **While doing practical work, make notes in a book.** A 'rough' book is far better than odd sheets of loose paper – you're less likely to lose parts of your notes if they're in a book.

3 **Write down your observations.** Write down exactly what you see – even when you don't yet know what it means. Don't depend on your memory.

4 **Find out exactly what sort of report or 'write-up' is required or expected.** Research your tutors' tastes in report presentation.

5 **Write your report 'same day' when possible.** It's far easier (and safer) to write your report while you still remember exactly what you did, and what you observed.

6   **Draft the 'central' parts of your report first.** These 'central parts' normally include sections such as 'method' or 'procedure', 'observations', 'data', 'analysis of data' and so on.

7   **Pay particular attention to the interpretation of your findings.** When working out what your conclusions are, take into account sources of error. Explain any assumptions you make – better still, don't make assumptions.

8   Complete your report, **adding references to theory and comparisons between your findings and other data**. Explain any discrepancies or surprising results.

9   **Don't accumulate a backlog of practical reports.** When you've got several practical reports to write up, one practical session begins to merge with another in your mind. You could end up writing practical reports at a time when the job you should *really* be doing is getting down to some serious preparations for exams.

10 **Hand reports in on time** – even if you're still not satisfied with them. Don't be a perfectionist. A 'mediocre' report is likely to score half-marks at least – if you don't hand anything in you're certain to score exactly zero!

Maximizing Your Tutorials

A tutorial is a less formal occasion than a lecture. One-to-one tutorials are useful – but rare. Normally you'll be in a small group for tutorials. The danger is that because tutorials are less formal, you can be lulled into treating them casually. The following suggestions can help you derive substantial benefits from tutorials as part of your studies.

1   **Take tutorials seriously** – then your tutors will too! Attendance counts – absence is noticed, and won't do you any good.
2   **Tutorials are examinable!** You're likely to get exam questions on things you did in tutorials that you didn't cover in any other way. They are part of your learning menu.
3   **Prepare for each tutorial.** Go over things you've covered so far. Try to find out whether there's an agenda for the tutorial.
4   **Store up questions.** Tutorials are often the best occasions to ask your tutors questions that you wouldn't ask in lectures. Tutors may have more time to explain things and give examples in tutorials.
5   **Keep a log of your tutorials.** Notetaking may not be normal – depending what sort of tutorials you have. However, it only takes a few minutes *after* each tutorial

to jot down a few things you've just learned. Also, jot down questions that were discussed – your questions, and other people's questions.

6 **Contribute positively.** Don't just sit back. Your contribution gets noticed and can make an important impression on your tutors. Build relationships with your tutors. You may need their support later – for example as referees when you apply for jobs.

7 **Use tutorials to help you find out exactly what's expected of you.** Tutorials are occasions when you can gain an insight into how the examiners' minds work.

8 **Find out how you're doing, compared to other people.** Tutorials provide a useful frame of reference.

9 **Reward 'good tutoring'.** When tutors provide valuable tutorials, let them know how much you appreciate them. This leads to more 'good tutorials'.

10 **Accept feedback.** Don't resort to trying to defend yourself, or explaining what you were trying to do. Defensiveness inhibits further feedback. All feedback is useful – even when it's a bit painful. You can learn from all feedback – positive and negative alike.

Getting the most from Field Courses

Field courses are often like extended practical classes. They often take the form of a residential course away from college. It may be an enjoyable holiday in many respects – but it's worth maximizing the potential benefits as the following suggestions show.

1 **Find out all you can.** Find out about the purposes of the course. Find out what you'll need to take with you. Try to find someone who has already been on a similar course, and find out what may be in store for you.
2 **Find out if it is assessed, and if so – how.** Check whether things you may learn during the field course may be asked for in later exams.
3 **Revise before it starts.** You'll get more out of a field course if you know what you're doing. You'll also be less likely to make a fool of yourself!
4 **Keep a log.** Valuable things can be forgotten quickly – especially when you may do all sorts of new things in a short time. Jot down notes frequently – just enough to remind you of things you may need to remember – and things you may wish to follow-up later. Even better, work informally as part of a small group keeping a group-log.
5 **Use the occasion to develop skills which employers**

value. Improve your skills at working with other people. Take any chances to develop leadership skills.

6 **Make notes of things you don't understand.** You may not have time to do anything about some of these while on the field course, but if you can remember what the questions were, you can find out the answers later.

7 **Find some kindred spirits.** A field course is a useful occasion to find some fellow students that you can continue to work productively with later.

8 If a report is required, **make daily notes of things you may use in it.** Then write it up as soon as possible after the course finishes – when you can still remember exactly what your notes mean!

9 **Build relationships with tutors.** You may need them later as referees. A field course is a good occasion to 'get on the right side' of your tutors – they may then be more likely to give you support if you need it – for example if you're a 'borderline case' at an exam board.

Build relationships with tutors

10 **Be philosophical in adversity!** Meals, accommodation and so on will not be 'perfect' for everyone – or for anyone. You can survive temporary deprivation or inconvenience. You'll need your survival skills again – develop them.

Using Vacations

Suddenly, the pressure is off. There is an understandable temptation to do precisely nothing! Vacations can, however, prove to be the most valuable part of your studies – if you take charge of them rather than letting them take charge of you. The following suggestions give some ways of making vacations satisfying and productive.

1   **Plan a rest – but don't have it yet!** In fact, you can start making your vacation productive even before it starts – terms usually 'fizzle out' before they end, and you can be doing things while most of your colleagues are doing little.

2   **Do any set 'vacation work' in the first week** (or before the vacation starts). Don't spoil your vacation by leaving work till the last week – and spending a lot of time thinking about it. Doing vacation work early is more efficient – you still remember the things you've been learning.

3   **Do something useful that you could not do during term time.** Earn some money – or get some experience – something useful to put in your CV if possible. Or learn to use a word processor – something that will save you time and money later.

4   **Use the lack of interruptions.** You can learn more in

vacations, (even if you're doing a vacation job) uninterrupted by lectures, tutorials or deadlines. There's no need to stop learning just because the teaching has stopped – most learning has little to do with teaching anyway!

5 **Reflect.** It's an important part of the way we learn things to look back at them and think around them – there's not nearly enough time for this vital process during term time. Look at things you've mastered – and things you've not yet mastered.

6 **Look back at your study strategy.** Make resolutions if you find any weaknesses. Tell other people about your resolutions.

7 **Practise things you can already do.** Keep your abilities polished – you'll need them again.

8 **Start on next term's agenda.** Find out what you already know about subjects which will be coming up next term. Find out exactly what you don't yet know – so you'll be receptive to it as it unfolds in the coming term.

9 **Explore some of the interesting things you didn't have time for earlier.** Vacations are the best time to

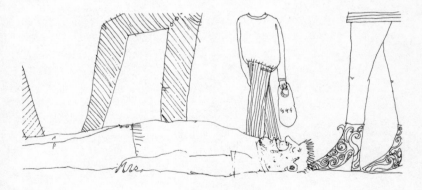

Have that rest!

enjoy the luxury of running off at tangents for a while.

10 **Have that rest!** The break will be all the more satisfying when you know that you've done a fair amount of work – and especially enjoyable when you've not got any particular tasks still waiting to be started.

Passing Vivas

'Viva' (from *'Viva voce'*) usually means an 'oral' exam. In practical terms, it means being put 'on the spot'! Vivas are used for several different purposes, including judgement of 'borderline' cases from exams, part of the examination system leading to higher degrees. It's a sort of civilized trial by ordeal! The following suggestions may help you make it less of an ordeal.

1   **Don't just hope 'it'll be all right on the day'!** There's a lot you can do to prepare for your viva constructively, as shown below.

2   **Look particularly at things you know you were weak at.** This is particularly appropriate when your viva represents a follow-up to exam results – often a second chance. The examiner(s) will probably probe you on the areas of weakness – if you show that you've overcome the weakness, your chances are improved dramatically.

3   **Make a long list of questions you could be asked.** In a viva, your ability to answer questions is to be tested – the more you can work out about what the questions may be, the better equipped you can go into the viva.

4   **Practise giving *spoken* answers.** Use the list of questions you prepared – get other people to quiz you with

them if you can. The more *practised* you are at answering questions in speech, the better you will perform at any viva.

5 **Don't 'invent' an answer when you've no idea.** Examiners conducting vivas don't like to be made fools of! It's better to admit when you don't know something – then perhaps advance a guess – but *calling* it a guess.

6 **Regard a viva as an opportunity to *improve* your score or grade.** Vivas are seldom used to 'pull a candidate down'. If you're on a borderline, the viva may be a chance for you to demonstrate that you should be pulled up over it. Alternatively, you may get a viva when you're typical of a candidate 'in the middle' of a range – in this you're simply being used as a 'reference'.

7 **Don't alienate the questioner.** Listen carefully to questions. Be receptive to body language, tone of voice and so on. Tune in to any 'vibrations' you feel as you answer questions. You can often tell quite quickly when you're on the wrong track.

8 **Demonstrate confidence.** The overall impression counts a lot. If for much of the viva you're giving correct answers confidently, you build up a good overall impression. So when you know something well, make sure that your confidence in yourself shows.

9 **Let other people talk too.** When you've got a viva, you may have one or more examiner trying to talk. Every second they talk is a second *less* for you to have to talk! So *don't* finish their sentences for them or cut them off in their prime!

10 **Minimize silences.** If there's a pause, try to avoid it becoming an uncomfortable silence. Explain a little more about the last answer you gave. Rephrase it. But remember that what seems like a long silence to you

(for example while you're thinking how to express an answer to a question) is probably quite short in fact.

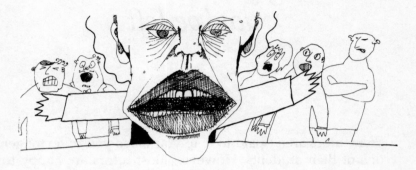

Let other people talk too

Using your Tutors after you've left

Your tutors aren't paid to help you when you're no longer one of their students. However, most tutors are happy to continue to help – if you've prepared them well and if you approach them in the right manner. The following suggestions can help you make the most of your tutors – even years after you've left your studies.

1 **Prepare the ground** – establish a good relationship with those tutors whom you may need help from later.
2 **Ask their permission** – for example when you wish to use them as referees in job applications. You're not going to get a good reference from tutors who have to rack their brains to try to remember whether they said they would act as referees.
3 **Find out who's experienced at giving references.** Giving a good reference is a skill. Some tutors are well-practised at it – others aren't. Departmental Secretaries (who often type the references) may be willing to advise you which tutors to 'cultivate' for this purpose.
4 **Keep them informed.** If you're using a tutor as a referee for example, supply written information about the jobs you're applying for. References are often required at very short notice – sometimes referees will be telephoned by employers. If a tutor knows what you're

applying for, it's possible to be ready to give help at short notice.

5 **When asking advice, ask clear questions.** There may be occasions later in your career when a former tutor is a good person to advise you on a situation. Don't make it hard for the tutor to work out exactly what you're asking.

6 **Remember to thank them.** It's easy to be so preoccupied with the matter you're seeking former tutors' help on, that you forget the simple courtesy of thanking them! Tutors will notice when they're being taken for granted.

7 **Don't telephone them out of the blue.** (And definitely don't turn up on your tutor's home doorstep with a suitcase – as one of my former

Don't turn up on your tutor's doorstep with your suitcases

103

students did to me!!) Tempting as it is to pick up the phone and contact former tutors when you need their help, don't forget they're in the middle of *their* lives. They can't just drop everything and respond to your needs. An advantage of writing rather than telephoning is that they can deal with your requests at a time which suits them. Alternatively, you can arrange with a tutor a 'telephone appointment'.

8 **Keep contacts going – make your former tutors feel valued.** Most tutors are glad to be kept informed of the careers of former students. Postcards from exotic places can create interest!

9 **Offer something in return.** This is not meant to be taken as an invitation to 'bribe' your former tutors! However, offering to return to college to talk to present students about your experiences could be welcome.

10 **Send tutors information they could use with their present students.** Tutors are often on the lookout for relevant case-study information.

Using Advice

At times, you may feel that there's far too much advice coming your way! This *could* mean you may need to review your attitude towards advice – the following suggestions may help you to decide whether you need to do this.

1 **Regard all advice as valuable** but not necessarily 'right'. Advice is often based upon other people's experiences – and their mistakes – **you** may be able to learn from both.

2 **Don't go on the defensive.** The moment you become defensive, you're likely to stem the flow of advice. This could mean missing out on some really useful advice which may be on the way.

3 **Keep track of whose advice proves really useful.** Seek more advice from those people who seem to give you the best advice. It's useful to build up your own network of people you can trust, and seek their advice when you need help in reaching decisions about courses of action.

4 **Thank people for their advice.** Thank them even when you don't take their advice. Just because you're not taking on board one particular piece of advice doesn't mean you are ignoring it – or that you won't use the next piece of advice.

Thank people for their advice

5 **Get alternative advice.** It's often useful to see what the consensus of opinion is. Don't just stop when you've found some advice you like – see if there are any further ways of looking at the situation – then make your choice.

6 **Expose yourself to advice – don't hide from it.** Open channels of communication to people who may have good advice to offer you. Overcome the temptation to rush in to the course of action you instinctively prefer – at least until you've had the chance to weigh up the advantages and disadvantages of particular courses of action.

7 **You're still ultimately in charge.** Advice is only **advice.** You still need to take the responsibility for deciding which advice is worth heeding.

8 **Be willing to positively seek advice.** When you *seek*

106

advice, you're under rather more of an obligation either to take it – or at least to consider it very carefully. Work out when you need to seek advice – don't try to solve every problem on your own.

9   **Regard advice as a source of opportunities** – some of which would not have come to you on their own.

10 **Learn** from the occasions when you follow the wrong advice. Don't transfer the blame to the people who advised you, however. It was still *your* decision to follow the advice.

Revision

Revision is the most important study-activity you can do if you're going to be measured by exams. If you'd started systematic revision months ago, you wouldn't feel under any pressure now. *But forget what you didn't do*, you've got control only over the time that is left. The following suggestions can help you maximize the time between now and your exams.

1 It's the **quality** of your revision that counts – not just the quantity. Keep track of how productively it's going – not just how long it's lasting.
2 Practise **answering questions**. Exams measure your ability to answer questions. The more you've practised, the easier it becomes.
3 **Make your own lists** of questions to practise with. Hundreds of short, sharp questions are best. Get other people – anyone – to quiz you with your questions. Work **with** fellow students – not against them.
4 Regard it as **good news** every time you come across something you've forgotten or can't yet do. Once you know exactly what might have been a trouble spot, you're in a position to tackle it. It's when you don't know what you don't know, that you may never know!
5 Don't write out full answers every time you practise

answering questions. Map out some of the answers in **skeleton form** – you can cover more questions that way.

6 **Don't kid yourself** that if you're reading something you're revising it. Reading is dangerously passive. Keep reading to a minimum, and do more active things.

7 **Make summaries of everything** as you read and revise. Then work with the summaries, and mentally try to reconstruct some of the detail of the original. Whittle down what you've got to learn to manageable proportions.

8 Revise everything **often, not just once**. The more often something has been through your mind, the better you'll understand it and remember it.

9 Work in **short, sharp spells** with breaks in between. Concentration spans last for minutes, not hours. Active learning can't go on for hours on end, (only such routine tasks as essays or reports can be done continuously for hours).

10 As the exam gets near, concentrate on **polishing** up things you already know, rather than tackling the unknown.

A final reminder: it's not just what you know that counts. It's how well you can answer exam questions that will determine your results. So it all boils down to how well practised you can become – *so get practising!*

Making Projects Productive

A **Project** is normally an extended piece of work, leading to a dissertation, report, or presentation (or more than one of these), which occupies a substantial place towards the end of a programme of studies. It normally has to be 'passed' at least. The following suggestions will alert you to some ways of tackling projects – and avoiding some of the dangers associated with them.

1 **Find out what the Project's worth.** They're usually worth a substantial number of marks – but the main danger could be *spending too much time on it*. It's not uncommon for a student to spend so much time on a project that there's no time left for vital revision before exams. A project which gains a 'distinction' is no compensation for some failed exams.

2 **Start it at once!** A project tends to be a big task – and it's easy to find ways of avoiding the evil moment of getting started on it. It can be put off for months! Obviously, at the beginning you haven't assembled all the information you'll need – but that's no reason for not starting it.

3 **Plan it.** Break the project down into a series of much shorter tasks and activities. Keep your plan flexible so that when you discover new and important aspects,

Find out how much your project's worth

you can build them in as you go along. A good way of
starting on the plan is to 'brainstorm' (a) things you
already know, and (b) things you'll need to find out.
Then decide what order you'll attempt the first few
steps.

4   **Spend a little time on it every day** – at least up to the
time where you've got a complete first draft. Set aside
(for example) a 'project half-hour' and stick to it –
don't exceed it and don't skip it. This means that not
only do you make steady and regular progress on your
project, but you also keep up with all the other things
you need to be doing.

5   **Make use of help.** Your tutors may be willing to give
you suggestions – listen, avoid being dogmatic about
your own ideas. Library staff may be able to offer

111

valuable help in tracking down relevant information – let them see how much you appreciate such help. All sorts of people (fellow students, friends, employers, acquaintances) may have valuable suggestions – if you approach them the right way and make their help 'valued'.

6 **Get a very early first draft.** The longer you have a draft version of the entire project, the more you can work it up and improve it. The final version may end up being your 14th draft! Using a word processor throughout makes the whole business of revising and amending very efficient in terms of time and energy.

7 **Check continually that you're really 'addressing' the topic.** It's dangerously easy to get preoccupied with one or two particular strands, and to end up with a project which misses many key aspects.

8 **Put it in a drawer for a while!** The 'drawer' treatment is beneficial for many kinds of extended written work. When you return to it days or weeks later, you're able to read it in an objective way – similar to the way assessors will be reading it – and you're likely to find a number of important changes you can make. If you'd stayed 'too close' to it, you'd have missed the chance to see where some of these changes were needed.

9 **Seek feedback.** There will be other people who can give you critical comment before it's too late. Make sure you don't resort to defending what you've done, when someone is making suggestions. All criticism is useful – at the end of the day it is *you* who decides which critical comment you're going to heed.

10 **Submit it on time – or a little early.** Being punctual creates a good impression. Work which comes in late has usually been rushed – and those assessing it may start off with a negative view about it.

Using Old Exam Papers

Past exam papers can be one of your most valuable resources. The following suggestions may help you to make optimum use of them as you prepare for your own exams.

1 **Get them early.** Don't worry if you can't understand most of them at this stage. You can usually purchase old exam papers – or sometimes your tutors will be willing to give specimen papers to you. If you're on a new course, ask for specimen papers as a guide to the format and structure of the exams you should expect.

2 **Work out what the standards are.** For example, use the old exam papers to give you an idea about how much you've got to cover in an answer in half-an-hour, or how much to cover in a complete exam of three hours, and so on.

3 **Get to know what the questions may be** – even before you know any of the answers. The more you're tuned in to the nature of likely questions, the more receptive you are to the answers as you come across them in lectures, reading and studying.

4 **Break the old exam questions down.** Break them into lots of short, sharp questions. The aim is to be able to answer all the little bits out of which bigger questions are made.

5   **Try to work out the marking scheme.** As you become able to answer old exam questions, make lists of points which you think may have scored marks. Also, try to work out the most likely causes of *losing* marks on the questions – in order to avoid such things yourself later.

6   **Practise answering them.** In due course, your own exams will measure your skills at answering exam questions. This depends on how well practised you have become. Check how long it takes you to answer old questions – try to work your speed up gradually, until you can do such questions in the limited time that may be available in an exam.

7   **Find out which questions you're best at.** If you've got a choice of questions in your exams, it's useful to know which sorts of questions will prove 'safest'. This can save you spending too much time making choices in your exams.

8   **Practise 'skeleton answers'.** For example, practise spending 5 minutes mapping out how you would answer a 30-minute question. You can get through a lot more 'thinking' by making several skeleton answers than if you simply sat writing one 'full answer'.

9   **Work through some questions with fellow students.** Find out the things that they think of that you would have missed. Between you, work out what the best possible answer may be.

10 **Do some 'question-spotting'.** Note the trends. Note things than come up frequently. Also look for things that haven't come up recently and which may be 'due' for another airing. Remember, though, that question-spotting is a gamble – don't invest too much in it!

Before Your Exam

Getting to your seat in the exam room in the right frame of mind is a valuable start towards doing yourself justice in your exam. The following suggestions may help you to avoid some of the things that can lead to a shaky start.

1 Before the day of the exam, find out exactly **where** the exam room is. This is important if you've got exams in buildings you're not familiar with. It saves you spending vital energy looking for the right room on the day.

2 Before the day of the exam double-check exactly **when** each exam is. There is always someone who gets it wrong (for example turning up at 1400 when the exam was at 0930!) Timetables for exams sometimes change, so make sure that you've got the latest information – check with the Secretary in your Department.

3 The day before your exam (or earlier) **get together the things you'll need** during the exam (for example: pens, pencils, calculator – check battery, rubber, Tippex, highlighting pen, drawing instruments, etc., depending on the nature of the exam). Put them all in a folder or pencil case. Make it so that on the day of the exam you only have to pick one 'thing' up rather than expending valuable mental energy scrabbling around looking for the bits and pieces.

4 **Don't work too hard!** If you work all of the night before an exam, you may indeed know quite a lot – but you'll probably be too tired to read the questions properly – and you'll certainly be too tired to do the questions justice. You're measured on what you do during the exam itself – not the night before.

5 When doing your final revision, don't depress yourself by finding out all the things you still don't know. Concentrate on **polishing-up things you already know**, rather than trying to learn things you don't know.

6 **Get some rest!** Don't worry about sleep – rest is just as useful. No use lying awake worrying about not being able to sleep! Once you've stopped worrying about lack of sleep, you'll probably doze off anyway.

7 On the day of the exam, aim to **get there early**. Make sure you'll still have plenty of time if the car won't start, or if the train doesn't run, or if you miss the bus. Being late for an exam uses up a lot of valuable mental energy – save it – be early.

8 On the day of the exam, **try to avoid stressful situations**. Don't argue with your partner. Don't let yourself get angry. Don't let anyone make you feel hassled.

9 Immediately before your exam, it's best to avoid the cluster of people outside the exam room asking each other questions such as 'do you think there'll be a question on Sprocket's Theorem?' or 'can *you* understand Dr Jinks' stuff?' and so on. If you participate, you'll almost certainly get the feeling that everyone around you seems to know a lot more than you do. This is because your ears prick up every time you hear something you **don't** know – you hardly notice hearing things you do know.

10 As the starting time draws near, think of the things

you **can do**, not the things you can't do. Remember that it's quite easy to get the first half of the marks anyway.

At the Start of your Exam

The first few minutes of an exam can be the most nerve-racking – but they can also be the most valuable minutes – if you do sensible things during them. The following tips for the first ten to fifteen minutes should help you to make a calm and logical start to each of your exams. Most of these suggestions only take seconds to put into practice – but it's well worth taking the trouble to use them.

1 **Check you're looking at the correct exam paper!** Often, several exams are underway in the same room, and it's quite possible to be sitting down in front of some other course's exam paper – maybe a much harder paper than yours, and possibly on a subject you've not heard of (two or three seconds).

2 **Do the 'administrative' bits and pieces** – putting your name or candidate number, date and time of the exam, etc., on the various forms and exam booklets on your desk. However tense you feel you're unlikely to have forgotten your name, and you can probably get the date from your watch or from the question paper itself (half a minute).

3 **Check the instructions** on the paper to see whether it's divided into various sections, how many questions you have to do altogether, how many from particular

Check you're looking at the correct exam paper

sections, how much choice you have, whether or not all questions carry equal marks, whether there are any compulsory questions – and remind yourself how long you've got altogether (takes maybe half a minute – but quite a few candidates don't spend this vital time – and end up doing too many – or too few questions!)

4   **Work out a timetable** for the exam, based on how many questions you need to do. In your calculations, leave 15 minutes or so 'spare' for checking towards the end of the exam, and remember to subtract the ten or so minutes you're presently spending at the start. **Jot down** 'target start times' for each of the questions you will do – this saves cluttering your memory with unnecessary information (half a minute or so).

5   **If you've no choice of questions,** you may then wish to start with your first question – or you may wish to

work out first which question is the **best** one for you to start with (see '6' below).

6   **If you have a choice to make:** read each of the questions, in turn, *slowly, calmly, and more than once.* Decide which questions are 'possible' ones for you to attempt – where you know you can do *some* parts of them – mark them ✔. Decide which are 'bad' questions – mark them '✘'. And decide which are 'good' questions – mark them ✔✔ (spend several minutes on this).

7   **Ignore the fact that everyone around you is scribbling!** Many candidates rush in where angels fear to tread. They may have already scored a few marks with their first page – but you will have **saved** even more marks by investing in sensible choices and a logical strategy for the exam.

8   (Optional). At this stage, you may wish to jot down on paper key ideas connected with the questions you're going to do. This can save you worrying about losing ideas that came into your mind when you first read the question. If you decide to make such notes for each question, it may be necessary to go back to your timetable and adjust it accordingly for the extra few minutes you're spending at the start.

9   Choose to start with a **good** question – to give yourself the feeling that you're making real headway – but remember to watch the timing – good questions tend to overrun. Be concise.

10   **Re-read your first question** once more – and start addressing it.

Writing Your Exam Answers

In the previous list I've given some pointers for getting the most out of the first few minutes of your exam. In this list, we'll look at the main part of the exam – the business of writing answers and scoring marks. In a further list, we'll explore some things to do towards the end of an exam.

1 **Keep – within reason – to the timetable** you planned for the exam. If (for example) you've got 5 questions to attempt in 3 hours, each question should take about 30 minutes (allowing for the 'special' time at the start and finish of the exam).

2 If your time for a question runs out – and you think it will take more than 5 minutes to finish it off – leave a gap and move on to another question. (If you **know** you can finish it in less than five minutes, finish it). The questions most likely to overrun are the early ones – where you know a lot – later questions may well under-run, allowing you to spend additional time finishing off unfinished early questions.

3 **Read the questions carefully**. Work out what they really mean.Keep re-reading the questions as you answer them. This helps you avoid going off on tangents. More marks are lost in exams by candidates

121

going off on tangents, than by candidates not knowing what the right answers are!

4   Make sure that each of your answers **addresses** the question. Don't waste time and energy writing down things the question doesn't require you to do. (You can always add more detail later if you find you have genuine 'spare' time). Take careful note of key words in questions including 'how?', 'why?' , 'when?', 'what?', 'explain', 'discuss', 'compare', 'contrast', 'evaluate', 'deduce', 'prove that', 'show that', 'decide' and so on. Do exactly what the question asks.

5   If you get stuck – leave your planned timetable for the moment – and move on to another question that you feel more comfortable with. You can avoid mental blanks by **not** trying to force your brain to recall things that are temporarily unavailable to you.

6   For essay-type questions, spend the first few minutes **planning** your answer. This helps to make sure that the essay has a promising 'beginning', a coherent 'middle' and a convincing 'conclusion'. Planning your essay at the start also helps you to avoid missing out important ideas.

7   For numerical or problem-type questions, make sure the examiners can see **exactly how** you reached your answers. Show clearly each step you take. Show where you substituted numerical data into formulae. If something goes wrong, you can still get marks for all the things the examiners can **see** that were correct. If the examiners can't see where you went wrong, they can't give you any credit for those steps that were right.

8   **Try to keep your sentences short and simple**. Less can go wrong with short sentences – there's less chance of the examiners reading them the wrong way. Also, scripts that can be read easily help put examiners into a better mood – more generous with marks.

9   **Humour your examiners**. Make it easy for them to see where you've finished one question and started another. If they can find their way easily through your script, their generosity tends to increase.

10 Every now and then **give yourself a minute off**. Give your brain a chance to rest and reflect. Give your thoughts time to put themselves into a sensible pattern. Then write some of the sense down.

Near the End of Your Exam

It's possible to score more marks in the last quarter of an hour of your exam than you did in any other quarter of an hour. The following suggestions can help you pick up useful extra marks in this final stage of your exam.

1 **Don't leave early.** Ignore other candidates who walk out when they've finished the paper. If you walked out, the chances are that as soon as you left the exam room, you'd remember something important that you could have added to your answers.

2 **Stop answering the exam questions.** Even if you're still in the middle of a question, there are usually more marks to be gained by following the suggestions below, than by continuing trying to finish the question.

3 **Reading your script from beginning to end, do the activities explained in '4' , '5' and '6' below,** even though you won't feel like doing this – it may go against all your instincts.

4 As you read it through, make **corrections** – you'll notice quite a few things that weren't as you intended them to be. When candidates are allowed to see their scripts again, they can spot all sorts of things that they could have corrected – showing that few candidates ever took the sensible step of re-reading their answers.

5   As you read through your answers, also make **additions** – when important ideas have filtered into your mind *since* the time you wrote your answers. Your subconscious mind will have been continuously bringing forward ideas since the start of the exam – get the extra ideas down on paper where they can score marks.

6   As you read, make occasional **adjustments**, to make the meaning of key sentences and paragraphs easier for the examiner to follow.

7   If you happened to make a 'false start' at a question, make your intentions clear regarding which questions the examiners should take into account. If you were asked to answer five questions, examiners would otherwise mark only the **first five** questions you answered – such regulations are designed to prevent candidates from 'hedging their bets', trying to answer a bit of all the questions. A single line through a 'deleted' question is enough to make your intentions clear (and still allows a kind examiner to read the 'deleted' answer, if looking for a way to get your mark above a borderline).

8   When you've checked through the whole of your script as above, if you've still got time left, it may be worth **going back to any unfinished questions**, and trying to finish them off – possibly in note-form if time is really short.

9   If you've still got time left, do a bit of **tidying-up**. Make it easy for the examiner to find where each question starts and finishes. Make headings, main points and conclusions 'stand out' a little more.

10 **Stay at your desk till time is up**. Even in the last minute, an idea may come back to you, which is worth an extra mark or two.

After An Exam

After your **last** exam (or if you've only got **one** exam) – you can do whatever you want! However, if you've got more exams coming up shortly, doing the 'wrong' things after an exam can cause you to become so dispirited that you don't do yourself justice in your **next** exam. Some suggestions are given below, regarding do's and don't's for the time immediately after an exam.

1   Accept that the moment the exam finished, **that particular exam is completely out of your control**. Your script is now in the hands of the examiner.

2   **Avoid the 'post-mortem'**. Though it's instinctive to want to find out what your mark is likely to be, you can't change your mark. It's now up to the experts to work out your mark – there's nothing you can do to help them!

3   A post-mortem is likely to **demoralize** you rather than cheer you up! At a post-mortem, you'll find out things you got wrong or missed out. Even when you find things you got right, your mind will still be preoccupied with the things you find you got wrong.

4   Post-mortems are in any case a **complete waste of your time and energy**. Are exams so enjoyable that people want to re-live every nuance of the experience,

step by step, in slow motion? Students have been known to spend days going over a 3-hour exam!

5   After an exam, you're needing a rest – but aren't quite ready for it. You've got extra adrenalin in your system. So plan how you can **put this extra alertness to some sort of useful purpose.** Choose from some possibilities listed below.

6   **Do a little 'gentle' revision for your next exam.** This can give you the satisfying feeling that you're *'flushing out the old information from your brain, and replacing it with the new information you'll need next'*. It takes a fair amount of self-discipline to walk away from one exam and start immediately preparing for the next – but try it. You may feel so pleased with yourself that you'll turn it into a habit.

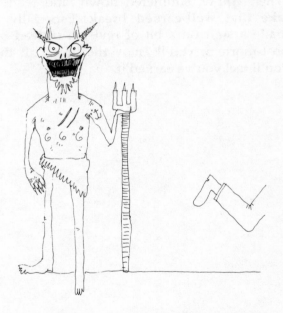

Stay away from people who would tempt you

7   **Do some general 'tidying up'** – preparing for the next subject you're going to be studying. Getting your books and papers for your next exam sorted out is much more enjoyable than doing the average post-mortem. Getting yourself organized ready for your next period of revision can help you save time later.

8   **Stay away from people who would tempt you** into talking about the exam that is over. Even if you're really curious to find out what the correct answer to question 5 actually was – resist the temptation. If you're still keen to find out – leave it till after your **last** exam.

9   **Do a bit of planning** about how best to use the time remaining before your next exam. Remember to build in some time for relaxation.

10 When you're 'simmered down' and ready to relax, **take that well-earned break**. Especially if you've made a start on a bit of revision instead of doing a post-mortem, you'll enjoy the break all the more – you'll feel you've earned it.

Preparing for your Re-sit

Preparing for a re-sit exam wasn't part of your plans! However, if you find yourself in this position, the most sensible thing to do is to prepare for it logically and constructively. The following suggestions can help you make the most of such situations.

1 **Accept the situation.** If you go about feeling resentful that you've got to re-sit one or more exams, it won't make your task any easier. It could have been worse – you may have had to repeat a whole year.
2 Regard the situation as a **positive opportunity** to learn things you haven't yet mastered quite well enough. You'll benefit from the extra knowledge and skills as you continue with the next phase of your planned studies. In fact, having 'fresher' knowledge and skills may launch you into the next phase of your studies with an advantage.
3 Look back objectively at **what went wrong with the revision** leading up to the unsuccessful exam. More than likely, you may have underestimated how long it would take you to master certain key parts of your subject. Possibly your revision was too 'passive' with not sufficient practice at answering exam questions.

Now's your chance to practise what you've learned from the experience.

4 Go carefully through the exam papers that caused you the problems. **Work out exactly what you didn't know.** Similar questions may come up again in a re-sit paper – sometimes identical questions have been known to appear again.

5 Look back objectively at the exams which caused the problems. Try to work out whether there were any **exam strategy weaknesses** which contributed to your problems. Did you mismanage the timing? Did you struggle too long with things you were 'stuck' on – and not notice other questions on the paper you could have done? If you had a choice, did you pick the best questions for you?

6 Look through the past exam paper for any important topics which **didn't** come up that time. The examiner designing the re-sit paper may be doing just that too! Look to previous years' exam papers for the sort of questions that were asked on these topics – as the examiner designing the paper may also be doing. Pay particular attention to questions and topics which your researches indicate may be hot favourites.

7 **Don't leave your revision a minute longer – start now!** Aim to cover all the material several times well before the date of the re-sit. Revision is less tense – and more productive – when it's not done under pressure.

8 Focus your revision on **practice at answering questions.** That's what you'll be doing when you take the re-sit – and practice makes perfect.

9 Aim firmly at getting a **comfortable pass** with the re-sit – not a distinction. During the exam, once you know you've passed comfortably, you can pull out any extra energy and aim higher.

10   If you can, spend some time **working with other people** who are preparing for the same re-sit exams. Quiz each other, work out possible questions with each other, share your analysis of what went wrong in the original exam – all this helps you learn actively from the situation you find yourself in.

Using a Word Processor

Learning to use a word processor can be a valuable invest-
ment in your future. It can save you time, saving you from
having to depend on typists and secretaries in future.
Being able to make 'professional-looking' reports, essays,
and dissertations can improve your chances of getting the
qualifications you want.

1   **Choose your system.** You may not have a choice of
    course! If you are in a position to choose what sort of
    word processor to acquire, talk to as many other peo-
    ple as you can who know about them – get them to let
    you have a go! It's worth finding out what 'fonts' and
    print-sizes are at your disposal. Most people prefer
    systems where the screen display is **'wysiwyg'** – 'what
    you see is what you get'. This means you can control
    the way your final print-out will appear.
2   **You won't break it!** Don't be frightened of the word
    processor. The **worst** thing that could happen to you
    (and probably will!) is that you may lose a long docu-
    ment. So start to develop the habit of 'saving' things
    regularly, and keep back-up copies of disks.
3   **Compose at the keyboard.** Just make skeletons on
    paper, and get the practice at the keyboard.
    Alternatively, many word-processor users don't bother

You won't break it – don't be afraid of the WP

writing anything on paper, they just sit and write at the keyboard directly.

4   **Learn by doing.** Use the word processor for notes, letter, essays, reports, projects, shopping lists – leading up to dissertations, theses, and books!

5   **Be prepared to ask.** When you get stuck – or when you don't quite know how to make it do what you want it to do, it's often far quicker to ask someone who knows. It can take ages to track down the information you need from instruction manuals.

6   **Keep records of your filenames.** This may sound obvious, but as time goes on you may have hundreds of files on disk – and it's very easy to forget what you called a report you did six months ago. Putting the month and year in the filename is quite useful, for example my filename for this book has **jy91** in it.

7　**Print out drafts, and edit on paper as well as on the screen.** There are things that you notice on paper that you miss on the screen – and vice-versa. Also, a printed draft is a life-saver if the worst happens – for example if you lose your document due to a power cut while 'saving' it.

8　**Learn to touch type.** Use a vacation, perhaps, to learn to type with **all** your fingers. There are several excellent typing-tutor computer programmes which you can use. Don't worry about making a lot of mistakes – you can edit them out afterwards. The real aim is to gain speed – it's possible for you to type far faster than you can write.

9　**Don't worry about spelling too much.** Many word-processing programmes have 'spellchecks' built in. These will pick up all the usual mistakes – and also will show many typographical errors. But of course, spellchecks can't tell you when you've mixed up 'there' and 'their' or 'weather' and 'whether'!

10　**Develop an eye for layout.** Don't just fill every page from top to bottom. Look for things that make a page look 'interesting'. Try to arrange that headings come at the top of a new page rather than at the bottom of a previous page. Experiment with the different type-faces (fonts) and sizes, **bold,** *italics* and so on.

Filling in Application Forms

When applying for jobs, you may fill in dozens of application forms – yet only be invited to interview for a handful of jobs. However, each form is important. Taking care with how you go about filling in the form can make all the difference. A well-completed application form serves the purpose of being an ambassador for you.

1 **Have up-to-date information to hand.** For example, keep an up-to-date Curriculum Vitae, so that you've got all important dates, addresses, referees, and so on collected in one place. Send a copy of your CV along with your application form (whether asked for or not).

2 **Copy the blank application form.** It's not usually possible to fill in an application form straightaway, without doing a bit of planning regarding how much information you can fit into the various boxes. Keep the 'real' form until you've finished experimenting.

3 **Watch for instructions such as 'black ink' or 'don't type'.** Usually, application forms will be photocopied when they get there – black photocopies much better than blue. Sometimes, personnel people want to analyse your handwriting for 'character traits', and then there will be an instruction to make sure that candidates hand-write their forms.

4 **Give an impression of being well-organized.** When you fill in your various qualifications, mention all the details, such as dates of examinations, examining boards, grades and so on.

5 **Highlight responsibilities you've held.** When giving details about your experience (including vacation jobs), make it particularly clear if you've held any positions of trust, or if you've been responsible for the work of other people.

6 **Fit information to the sizes of the boxes.** Don't squeeze a lot of information into a small box – you can always say 'for further detail, please see Curriculum Vitae enclosed'. Also, try to avoid leaving lots of blank space where boxes are too big for the information you have. Spin it out a bit!

7 **'Plant' some interview questions.** One way of doing this is by saying things about your interests and hobbies (in the appropriate box) which are interesting enough to be taken up by people who interview you. The more you can talk at your interview about things you know a lot about (such as hobbies), the more you'll give a positive impression.

8 **'Why should we appoint YOU?'** There's sometimes a question along these lines. Don't be too modest. It's all right to write something along the lines 'because I think my experience will enable me to do the job well'.

9 **Fill in the 'real' form carefully.** It's not easy to use word processors for pre-laid-out forms, so you'll either need to type it, or hand-write it. Either way, you don't want your form to give an impression of 'crossings-out' or 'Tippex'! Send a covering letter with the form, and a copy of your CV – making sure that there are no discrepancies between the information in your CV and that on your form.

10 **Keep a copy of the completed form.** When you've got several different applications in progress, it's easy to mix up what you said on one form with what you said on another. It's useful to look back at exactly what you said on your form if you're called to interview – that is the information your interviewers will be basing many of their questions on.

Writing your Curriculum Vitae

The advantage of your Curriculum Vitae is that you're in control of the style, size and layout (with application forms someone else controls all these). Your CV is meant to be an ambassador for **you**. You want your CV to give all the 'right impressions' about yourself. It's useful to have an up-to-date CV readily available all through your career – for internal use when seeking promotion, and for when better posts come up at short notice.

1 **Work out what you want your CV to do for you.** For example, you want it to give the impression of a well-organized person. You want it to be easy to follow. The main purpose of your CV is to serve as a passport to the shortlist.

2 **Factual information:** start your CV with information such as name, date of birth, nationality, address, marital status, and telephone number. It's better to give your date of birth than your age – your date of birth doesn't change, your age does! Make sure that it's easy for anyone reading your CV to contact you – if you haven't a telephone, try to find someone whose number you can use, and who can get messages to you quickly when necessary.

3 **Education and qualifications:** include as much detail

138

as may be wanted – for example dates, exam boards, contact addresses of most recent schools or colleges. Also include any **anticipated** qualifications, with dates you expect to be awarded them – making it clear of course that they are 'anticipated'.

4 **Employment and Experience:** (if you've got some – vacation jobs can be included) give sufficient detail of employers so that they can be contacted for further information about you. Make it clear whenever you have held positions of trust or responsibility. If you've been in full-time employment, it may be worth giving reasons for leaving.

5 **Career Aims:** it's useful to include a short section on these in your CV. Make it clear that you're not just looking for a lot of money for doing little work! Say **why** you're interested in things. Say **why** you think you will be good at things.

6 **Interests, hobbies, leisure, recreation** (don't use *all* these words as your subheading!). Use this section of your CV to make it clear that you're a 'normal', 'sociable', 'fit', and 'interesting' person. It's a useful place to 'plant' interview questions. Don't forget to mention any positions of responsibility you may have held in connection with your hobbies. Being president, secretary, treasurer or a committee-member of a club or society provides useful information about your skills.

7 **Update your CV regularly.** If you can, keep it on word-processor, so you can maintain control of the layout and appearance, and so that you can prepare a 'special edition' for particular applications.

8 **Choose the layout carefully.** You want your CV to give the impression that you are professional, well-organized, and interesting. This is easier if your CV is also professional, well-organized, and interesting. It also needs to be readable and easy to follow, with clear subheadings.

9 **Send a copy when you write for further information** (and another copy with your application form). Don't wait to be asked for your CV. If the *first* thing an employer sees about you is your CV, and if you're pigeon-holed at once as a worthy candidate, your application form will be taken more seriously in due course.

10 **Choose your referees.** It's best to quote three or so. Try to find people who look 'distinguished' , and who you can depend on to give you a good reference. **Ask them first.** Make it easy for firms to contact your referees – give telephone numbers as well as addresses. Referees are often contacted at short notice when a shortlist is being drawn up – getting on the shortlist may then depend on how easy *your* referees were to contact.

Preparing for an Interview

Some people hate interviews – others seem to thrive on them. The suggestions below may help you to prepare for interviews in ways that increase your chances – and increase your enjoyment.

1 **Become 'practised' at being interviewed.** Use friends, fellow students, relatives – anyone. Become used to answering questions on the spot. You can't become good at interviews simply by reading about them – it's something you learn best from experience.
2 **Don't get tense.** Plan to regard each interview as a learning experience. It's best if you can be 'laid-back' enough to regard being offered the job as a bonus rather than as a target. Then you're more likely to be offered the job!
3 **Prepare for 'tell us about yourself'.** Practise explaining your background, experience, and so on – so that you can keep going for five minutes if necessary. Don't expect people to have picked up all the details from your application form or CV – not every interviewer will have read them properly.
4 **Do a little research on the firm or organization.** This is particularly useful for helping you to be able to ask

some 'sensible' or 'informed' questions at your interview, when your turn to ask questions comes.

5   **Have some sensible questions of your own to ask.** Don't ask about money or holiday arrangements! Ask about training opportunities, the structure of the firm, and other things that make you seem to be a sincere, keen applicant.

6   **Be prepared for 'Why should we offer this post to you?'.** Be prepared to 'blow your trumpet' in a quiet but impressive way. Don't be embarrassed about your expertise and strengths.

7   **Before setting off for the interview, review exactly what you said on your application form** (and in your

Dress for the occasion

CV). Remember that this is the information they have about you (plus any further information your referees have supplied about you). Most of the interview questions will be based on this information.

8 **Plan your journey to arrive in good time.** Allow for any possible delay. You don't want to arrive for your interview flustered or breathless! Imagine the mental energy you'd have wasted if you spent half-an-hour knowing you were going to arrive late. Keep receipts for your travel expenses if you may be able to reclaim expenses after the interview.

9 **Dress for the occasion.** Use your judgement. Remember how important 'first impressions' can be. Interviewers really only have 'first impressions' to go on – so make sure that you give the impression you want.

10 **Be ready for anything!** You may have one-to-one informal chats, informal group discussions, one-to-one formal interviews – or a formal panel interview with a dozen people behind the table! Some interviews use psychological exercises and tests. Whatever you face, regard it as a chance to develop your experience – even if it doesn't 'pay off' this time.

Giving a Good Interview

There's no substitute for practice. Get all the practice you can to develop your interview skills. Make your primary aim at every interview to extend your experience of interviews. Don't expect to be offered every job you apply for.

1 **Be polite and friendly to everyone!** You don't know who people may be! The most impressive-looking member of an interviewing panel may not be the most important person there.

2 **If waiting with other candidates, don't let them make you feel inferior.** Sometimes candidates play a 'war of nerves' with each other, hoping to damage each other's chances. Don't be part of this. There may well be someone who is 'noticing' how candidates behave before the interview – for example a receptionist or secretary may be 'gathering extra information'.

3 **On entering – take your time!** Don't rush to the 'empty chair' and sit down too quickly. Soon enough you'll be 'motioned' to your seat and invited to sit down.

4 **Make eye contact.** For some people this is difficult to do – but anyone can develop eye-contact skills with practice. If looking people in the eye makes you feel uncomfortable, practise 'looking them in the eye but

144

not actually looking at them'! This is rather the same as learning to look a camera in the eye – you can't make real 'eye contact' with a camera – but you can appear to do so.

5 **Try to *appear* alert and confident – even when you don't feel it.** Most performers on 'live' television *look* calm and unflustered – but most will admit their pulse rate is up a lot until they 'get into their stride'. Yet they put on a good act of looking calm – so can you – with practice.

6 **Try to avoid silence.** In general, silence during an interview is a 'bad thing'! Try to find something to say – or something to ask – whenever a silence seems to be getting a bit too long.

7 **Don't interrupt.** Don't keep speaking when someone is trying to ask you something, or trying to respond to what you've said. If there's something you're desperate to tell your interviewers – wait – there will be another chance soon.

8 **Don't bluff.** When you don't know something, it's usually far safer to admit it straightaway, than to be 'found-out' after you've spouted a good deal of nonsense. 'I'm sorry, but I have not come across this yet' is better than saying something silly.

9 **Talk convincingly about what you know.** When you're on 'home ground' – such as when talking about your interests or hobbies – use the occasion to show your interviewers how you can be confident and enthused. This impression may carry over and help compensate for things you're less confident about.

10 **At panel interviews, talk to *everyone*.** Don't just reply to the person who asked you the last question – tell everyone. The person who asked you the question will probably know whether your answer is a good one – other people may not know. You may be able to

make other people feel you're giving a good answer. If you can impress most of the panel for most of the time – you're giving a good interview.

WHAT IS SCED?

SCED, the Standing Conference on Educational Development, is the principal organization in Britain for the encouragement of innovation and good practice in teaching and learning in Higher Education. It is essentially a co-operative network of colleagues from Universities and Colleges who want to make student learning more enriching and effective, working with the following broad aims:

- to lead and support the development of effective means of improving the quality of educational experience for students
- to provide a forum for discussion and for collaboration on creative ideas for learning development
- to assist the professional and personal development of lectures and educational developers
- to encourage greater understanding of the nature of student learning
- to offer support to new entrants to the profession
- to enable exchange of information and dissemination of good practice

The organization has grown from an informal network of practitioners to its current status as a focus of activity in the field of educational development. In the past, communications were relatively informal, but growth has led to a major reorganization. This makes the administration more efficient and enables exchange of information, dissemination of good practice and effective interactions of supportive colleagues, and recognizes especially the need for universities and colleges to co-operate more closely.

For further details and a list of SCED's other publications, please contact Jill Brookes, SCED Administrator, 69 Cotton Lane, Moseley, Birmingham B13 9SE.